The "Children Of Perestroika" Come Of Age

Also by Deborah Adelman

The "Children of Perestroika"
Moscow Teenagers Talk About Their Lives and the Future

The "Children Of Perestroika" Come Of Age

Young People Of Moscow Talk About Life in the New Russia

Deborah Adelman

M.E. Sharpe
Armonk, NY
London, England

Cover photo by Igor Timoshenko

Photographs on the following pages were taken by Deborah Adelman:
118
Photographs on the following pages were taken by Aleksandr Efremov:
16, 56, 106, 166, 174
Photographs on the following pages were taken by Igor Timoshenko:
36, 82, 98, 132, 142
Narratives translated by Deborah Adelman

Copyright © 1994 by Deborah Adelman

Library of Congress Cataloging-in-Publication Data

Adelman, Deborah.
The "Children of Perestroika" come of age : young people of
Moscow talk about life in the new Russia / by Deborah Adelman.
    p.   cm.
Includes index.
ISBN 1-56324-286-9   ISBN 1-56324-287-7 (p)
1. Young adults—Russia (Federation)—Moscow—Attitudes.
2. Youth—Russia (Federation)—Interviews.
3. Russia (Federation)—Social conditions.
I. Title.
HQ799.8.R92M68   1993
305.23′5′0947—dc20
90-10936
CIP

Printed in the United States of America

The paper used in this publication meets the minimum
requirements of American National Standard for Information
Sciences—Permanence of Paper for Printed Library Materials,
ANSI Z39.48-1984.

∞

BM (c)   10   9   8   7   6   5   4   3   2   1
BM (p)   10   9   8   7   6   5   4   3   2

For the new generation:
Andre, Gabriel, Glenna, Lucas, and Maya Florence

Contents

Preface

In 1989 I had the opportunity to spend six months conducting in-depth interviews with a group of Moscow teenagers, fifteen to eighteen years old, from diverse backgrounds. The interviews, published in 1991 in *The "Children of Perestroika,"* offered a view of life in Moscow during a period of radical change as seen through the eyes of adolescents. My conversations with these young people covered a wide range of topics, including family relationships, economic and political reform, and the teens' hopes and expectations for their own future and the future of their country, at that time still the Soviet Union.

I was curious about general issues such as family, intergenerational, and male-female relationships; leisure and recreational activities; hopes and desires for the future; and the degree to which the teenagers felt empowered to determine what their lives would become. But I was equally interested in discovering the specific issues that Soviet teenagers faced in 1989, especially the effects of *glasnost* and *perestroika** on their lives and thinking. During the time I spent getting to know these teenagers, in their schools and homes, accompanying them on excursions in Moscow and beyond, I was impressed by their excitement about the changes occurring in their country and their developing involvement with urgent social and political issues. But their eagerness to discuss their country and the events unfolding within it was

*The reader will find explanations of these and other special terms in the glossary.

matched by a realistic assessment of the problems that lay ahead. Although many of the teenagers felt that their generation was already quite different from preceding ones, they viewed perestroika and glasnost as the beginning of a long process of change, and identified themselves and their peers as representatives of that beginning. They described themselves as more involved and less afraid than their parents' generation, but perhaps not quite yet "children of perestroika." Theirs is a generation caught between rejection of the old ways and a full embrace of the new.

The eleven teenagers came from variety of social backgrounds and had different career and work aspirations at the time of the interviews. Some of the teens were studying in general academic schools, while others had enrolled in the vocational schools that prepare young workers to enter industrial jobs upon graduation. The difference between these types of schooling is significant. The choice between an academic or technical-vocational track, made upon completion of the ninth grade,* has long-term ramifications for students. Academic-track graduates prepare to enter an institute of higher education. Technical-vocational students train for white- and blue-collar occupations while simultaneously completing the universal secondary curriculum and are expected to enter the work force upon graduation. Vocational education is stigmatized, and students often end up in vocational schools on account of disciplinary or social problems rather than a commitment to any particular trade. Vocational students have the reputation of being unmotivated low achievers. In the group of eleven teenagers, four were attending vocational school. At the time of the interviews—close to graduation—they faced immediate job assignments and military service, all of which they considered highly undesirable. The teenagers attending academic high schools were planning to pursue a higher education and were worried about the highly competitive entrance examinations they faced.

---

*Secondary education extends to the eleventh grade.

Gender differences also proved to be important. The boys' views of male-female relations in general and their own future family relations were without exception patriarchal. Most of them felt that women should not work at all or that a woman should work only if she chooses to, but in that case she still must bear the primary responsibility for child-raising. The boys felt that it is a man's responsibility to provide for the family. But the girls all had educational and career aspirations, and although many agreed in principle that men should be the main providers for the family, they had no intentions of staying home to raise children and becoming dependent upon a husband. The girls in particular were aware of the double burden placed upon Soviet women—full participation in the work force, along with the major responsibility for housework and child care in a society with scarce consumer amenities.

Despite their many differences, however, all the teenagers were caught up in the major events occurring in the Soviet Union, whether they fully supported the changes or not. With rare exceptions, the teenagers showed striking awareness and interest in political and social developments.

In the summer of 1992 I returned to post-Soviet Moscow to meet with the teenagers and find out how the tumultuous changes that had taken place in the past three years had affected their lives and their plans for the future. I also wanted to bring each young person a copy of The "Children of Perestroika," which they had been eagerly awaiting. It was not my intention to conduct another series of interviews since I believed that some years would still have to pass before these teenagers would find their place in adult society. But I arrived to discover that tremendously important events had taken place in these young people's lives and had placed them squarely in the middle of adult life: they faced important decisions about work, career, marriage, and children; they were experiencing the rising social tensions and economic difficulties of their country directly. What I had expected to be brief conversations to "catch up" on events in their lives turned into lengthy, animated discussions revealing both disillusionment and hope. The young people express bitterness about failing new economic policies and increasing poverty and crime, but at the same time they still believe that the lives of ordinary Russians can improve and, more important, that they can personally play some role in ensuring that outcome. The excitement and enthusiasm I had found three years earlier were gone, but they had not been replaced with indifference.

Upon returning to the United States, I reviewed the taped interviews and was struck by the breadth of post-perestroika experience they contain. There are great differences in the ways each of these young people and their families are coping with the changes taking place in their country. For some the changes have meant greater economic hardship than for others. Some are having an easier time accepting new attitudes toward work, study, and the importance of making large amounts of money. Some have turned to religion to replace Soviet ideology and the values it represented, although baptism and church attendance have not been accompanied by an exploration of church doctrine or Christianity and Christian tradition in general.

In their often ambivalent attitudes about work, military service, religion, higher education, and lifestyle choices, these young people reveal a generation still caught between the old and the new, a generation not yet ready to abandon totally the values and attitudes that are part of the Soviet legacy, yet also not ready or sure how to incorporate themselves fully into a new way of life—especially economic life—in the new Russia. Their stories thus once again offer us an intimate view of life at a remarkably dynamic and volatile moment of Russian history.

Summer 1993

Acknowledgments

First and foremost I wish to thank the eleven young adults whose stories are told in this book. They took time from busy schedules to talk and write to me, even though it meant less time devoted to more urgent matters—studying for final exams at the university, taking care of a spouse confined to bed, trying to avoid the collapse of a business, and even missing a date or two. Special thanks are also due to the Gordon/Moralev/Tarkovsky family, who made the trip to Moscow possible and took me in as one of their own.

My editor at M.E. Sharpe, Patricia Kolb, gave the initial suggestion to write up material from the new interviews, and her enthusiastic response turned this into a book.

John T. Cabral read the manuscript in progress and offered helpful critical commentary. Anne Meisenzahl helped me sort through the issues raised by the new interviews when I first returned from Moscow.

And of course thanks to John and Norm for the many hours of child care that allowed me to finish this manuscript, and to Sharon and Reinaldo for being there for me during all the events, large and small, that took place during the time I was writing this book.

From Teenagers to Young Adults, 1989–1992

TANYA

In 1989, at the age of sixteen, Tanya was already planning a career as a teacher. From a working-class family, Tanya spoke of joining the ranks of the "workers' intelligentsia," which she viewed as a necessary link between workers and intellectuals. Class mobility and the gulf between workers and professionals were important issues for Tanya when she decided on a career in teaching.

Now nineteen, Tanya has finished her second year at a new experimental pedagogical college, where she is studying to become a primary-school teacher. She has one more year of studies to complete her training.

Tanya planned to marry her boyfriend, Seryozha, in September 1992. Seryozha is finishing his studies at a military school in Moscow, where he is training to become a border guard.

OLYA

In 1989, just short her eighteenth birthday, Olya graduated from a vocational school, where she completed her secondary education and was trained as a printer in a polygraphics factory. Upon graduation, an unhappy Olya received a two-year work assignment at the same factory. Although it had been Olya's decision to leave the academic track after the ninth grade,* by the time she graduated vocational school three years later she had come to regret her choice. She felt that she had made it at an age when she did not understand its implications for her future.

Avoiding the work assignment, Olya made several attempts to find satisfying work and eventually took a clerical position at a transportation agency, where she has been working for a year and a half.

Olya's mother is a factory worker who moved from a provincial city in order to marry. Olya's father is a construction worker, not steadily employed. When I met Olya in 1989, her parents had recently divorced. The family continues to live in the same apartment together, however, due to the complications of Moscow's severe housing shortage and Olya's father's refusal to leave the family home and take a room in a communal apartment,† which has been the only possible alternative.

LENA

Lena, at sixteen, was quite excited about glasnost and the process of perestroika. During her last year of secondary school she participated in numerous demonstrations and experienced a political awakening.

Lena took the competitive entrance exams to enter Moscow State University's School of Journalism immediately upon graduating secondary school. She was not accepted on her first attempt and had to wait a year until she could try again. In the meantime, she took a job as a correspondent for a small newspaper to help prepare her for the next

---

*For clarification of educational terms, please see the glossary.

†Communal apartments house two or more families, each family residing in a separate room but sharing kitchen and bathroom facilities. Communal apartments are generally found in old, run-down, unrenovated buildings and are one of the least desirable forms of housing. Their continued existence is indicative of the severe housing shortage that plagued the Soviet Union and continues into the present.

exams. Her second exams gained her entrance into the correspondence section of the School of Journalism. She continues to work, at a new job in a film studio, while she pursues
her studies. Now nineteen, Lena has finished one year at
Moscow State.

Lena's father is a film director for television. Her mother,
also a film director by training, produces programs for a
radio station.

ILYA

In 1989, at seventeen, Ilya was completing his secondary education at one of Moscow's elite special English schools and was
working hard to gain admission to Moscow State University.
An avid reader and well informed about the developments in
his country, he could already be considered a "Moscow intellectual." Ilya noted that his family is Jewish and that he had
been raised in dissident circles. He proudly considered himself
a progressive and independent thinker. He identified himself
as a supporter of the Soviet "opposition," the reformers who
were working to move the country toward a market economy.

Now nineteen, Ilya has finished his third year of studies in
the Department of Russian Language and Literature at
Moscow State University. In 1991 he married Sasha, a class-
mate from Moscow State. Ilya and Sasha were expecting a
child in October 1992.

Ilya's family circumstances have changed quite significantly
in the three years since our first interviews. His mother, an
economist and researcher, was killed. His older sister emigrated to Israel and plans to join her fiancé, who is on a
scholarship and studying at a university, in the United States.
His father, a renowned psychiatrist and poet, lives alone.

MAXIM

When I met sixteen-year-old Maxim he was studying to
become a chef. He had completed the ninth grade and then

dropped out of school in order to attend culinary school in the restaurant of the Hotel Moscow. In 1989, Maxim spoke of his eagerness to begin the military service required of all eighteen-year-old males, which he felt would help him mature and become disciplined. He hoped to be accepted into the navy, where he wanted to work as a chef on a ship.

Maxim comes from a working-class family. At sixteen Maxim's views conveyed the conservative social and political thinking that many considered to be most representative of the working class, which was less supportive of Gorbachev and his policies than were intellectuals and professionals.

Maxim's father used to work as a trainer for a professional soccer team but now works in a neighborhood health and recreation complex that runs a café and Russian sauna. His mother is a hairdresser in a beauty salon. The family lives in a communal apartment, which means that Maxim, his two younger sisters, and his parents share one room in an apartment inhabited by two other adults who have no relation to the family. In order to gain some privacy and independence, Maxim has spent much of the past three years living with his grandmother, who has a larger apartment in a different neighborhood, and more recently, with friends.

Now eighteen, Maxim finished his course at the culinary school and worked as a cook for almost two years, first in a hotel and then in the cafeteria of a government ministry. Despite his former enthusiasm for military service, he received a deferral and since that time has spent almost a year without any type of employment.

YELENA

As a sixteen-year-old ninth-grade student, Yelena became absorbed by her country's political changes and began to participate in public demonstrations. The political upheaval in her country deepened her interest in its history and led her to decide to pursue studies in a pedagogical institute or university and eventually teach history.

Yelena is the daughter of factory workers. In 1989 she described them as more politically conservative than she and criticized them for the "quietness" with which they had raised her. She imagined that she would raise her own children in a different, more active manner. She noted that her parents "liked to sit at home too much." The secondary school she attended during the years of glasnost and perestroika, with its politically active principal and atmosphere of open dialogue, had a great impact on her. Unlike her parents, she was enthusiastic about the new ideas that were being discussed and believed they would become the essential catalyst for true economic reform.

Now nineteen, Yelena works at a production training center for students in the upper grades of secondary school (grades 9–11). She does clerical work at the center and also teaches typing and computer data entry.

Yelena has tried to gain admission to an institution of higher education three times but thus far has not passed the entrance exams. Although she enjoys her work, she wants to complete a higher education and is preparing to take exams again.

DIMA

In 1989, Dima, at eighteen, had just completed his secondary education at a vocational school where he learned to repair radio and electronic equipment, and was preparing to report for military service. He was raised in a working-class family and neighborhood. For Dima, perestroika and glasnost were fundamentally related to changes at the workplace and the need to motivate and raise the productivity of Soviet workers. He anticipated working in a cooperative after completing his military service.

Now twenty-one, Dima is currently living in Canada. After completing two and a half years of military service, he joined an agricultural project organized by a youth agency, designed to interest young people in becoming independent farmers.

The project involved an internship with Canadian farm families. Dima decided to stay in Canada, although the internship has ended, because several of the participants in the program have written to him since their return to Russia about obstacles the project is encountering in its next phase that may ultimately result in its discontinuation.

LYOSHA

Lyosha graduated at eighteen from a vocational school, where, in addition to finishing his general secondary education, he learned how to assemble radio and electronic equipment. At the time of his graduation in 1989 he spoke of his desire to continue studying and become an engineer.

Lyosha is from a working-class family. His parents, who moved to Moscow from a provincial town before he was born, are both factory workers. The family travels often to that town, and Lyosha noted that one of the major differences he felt between himself and his parents is that they are provincial, while he has been raised as a Muscovite.

Now twenty-one, Lyosha began his military duty after graduating from the vocational school in 1989. He received an early discharge after six months. Currently he is involved in the same agricultural project Dima joined. After three months in Canada, Lyosha returned to Moscow, took courses at an agricultural institute, and is now trying to establish a small farm outside the city on land rented from a state farm.

ALEXEI

Alexei studied in a vocational school, where he learned carpentry. When I met seventeen-year-old Alexei in 1989, his parents were in the African republic of Burundi, where they had been working for eight years as university instructors of Russian. As a young boy Alexei lived for a number of years with his parents in Mali. Later, when they began working in Burundi, he returned Moscow to live with his grandmother.

Alexei is from a university-educated professional family, but his lack of interest in school led him to leave the academic track for vocational school. He thus prepared to become a member of the working class, an unusual choice for someone of his background. In 1989 he felt uncertain about his future, characterizing himself as not yet "serious enough" to pursue a degree in higher education although he assumed that eventually he would. He dreamed about becoming a conductor on the Moscow subway.

Now twenty, Alexei graduated from vocational school and received a medical certificate that excused him from military service. Alexei has worked in various places since graduation. He is currently a co-owner of a small optical cooperative and has become something of an entrepreneur.

NATASHA

Natasha, at sixteen, was enrolled in a special ninth-grade class for students who were interested in becoming teachers. She worked for two years in her secondary school as an assistant to a first-grade teacher and found the work gratifying. She praised the experiment as one of the few concrete successes of perestroika and glasnost in her school, although she felt that adults were still reluctant to let children have input into programs or to have any real power.

Now nineteen, Natasha studies in the same pedagogical college that Tanya attends. She has completed her second year and has one more to finish her course of studies and be certified as a primary-school teacher. She feels that her mother's job as a nurse has inspired her to work with people.

In March 1992, Natasha married her boyfriend, Andrei. Natasha and Andrei were expecting a child in November 1992.

KATYA

Katya, at sixteen, was enrolled in the same special pedagogical class as Natasha. In her last year of school she decided that she did not want to work with children and instead felt drawn to a technical occupation, perhaps because of her parents' work as engineers.

Now nineteen, Katya has completed two years of study at the Moscow Aviation Institute, a prestigious school with a variety of departments. She plans to specialize in economics, and will begin taking courses in her field in her third year of studies.

The "Children Of Perestroika" Come Of Age

"CHILDREN OF THESE HUNGRY TIMES"

In the summer of 1992 I returned to a Moscow that looked very different from the city I had left in 1989. Driving from the airport across the city, I noticed the proliferation of vendors and commercial activity at nearly every square and metro station. The city streets were much busier and dirtier than they had been. The three friends who had met me at the airport all spoke at once, in a rush of emotion, describing new difficulties and going into great detail about the cost of food, clothing, newspapers, and so on. They were not very interested in talking about much else. The enthusiasm for change that had been so evident in the summer of 1989 seemed to have disappeared. Now there was almost a sense of dread for what might come next. "We don't read the newspapers anymore," one of my companions told me during that first ride from the airport, "because we're tired of hearing about all that, and it just gets worse. And besides they're too expensive. We can't afford a daily paper." The talk focused on economic difficulties as my friends remarked with extreme displeasure that they considered the street vending speculative and parasitic, and they blamed the vendors and their dubious activities for the abundant piles of flattened cardboard boxes, broken slats from wooden crates, and stacks of garbage lining so many streets, left there at the end of a day's sales.

As I walked the streets of Moscow in the following days, it seemed that the city had become one large flea market.

Around the metro stations long lines of elderly women stood impassively, holding up an odd and unpredictable assortment of goods ranging from packs of cigarettes or bags of potato chips to a single puppy, a knit sweater, or a box of high-quality chocolate candies absolutely unavailable in state stores. Men sold fish they had caught, lined up on a piece of paper, drying and shriveling in the open air and sun. Others displayed cartons of milk and various food products purchased at the back doors of state stores and resold at large markups on the street. Although people I knew complained about buying from these vendors and warned me not to, business on the street seemed to flourish. And although there are many new shops and kiosks in Moscow with a variety of previously unavailable goods, most of them sell at prices that the average citizen simply cannot afford.

As I met with friends and acquaintances, it became clear to me that life had undoubtedly gotten much more difficult for almost everybody I knew. People were anxious, exhausted, disgusted, and worried. On numerous occasions friends asked me to pardon them for their obsessive talk about the cost of living.

"After ten minutes of any conversation, the topic always turns to money," a friend said. "We're in a state of shock." She and her husband, who at fifty-eight and sixty-three had just retired, had seen their life savings, about 10,000 rubles, reduced to nothing after the January 1992 price increases. Before January, 10,000 rubles had been a large sum that could ensure long years of security. "We thought we'd be like rich people in our old age," my friend exclaimed, "but now our life savings would buy us three pairs of blue jeans! We need a new refrigerator, but even a tiny one costs at least 12,000. And it took us our whole lives to save that 10,000!"

On another occasion I sat in the kitchen of a close friend, Inna, helping to prepare a pizza for the six of us gathered in her home. Inna, who comes from a well-known family of artists and poets, was discussing the uselessness of poetry at the present moment. She talked about her son, now publishing his own verses, with a mixture of pride and impatience. "He's got a family to feed," Inna said. "Who needs poetry in these circumstances?"

I listened, grating cheese for the pizza, thinking about how three years earlier Inna had spoken only with excitement about her son's developing talent. Suddenly the other woman present, an accomplished classical pianist, interrupted the conversation with a gasp. She pointed to the tiny piece of cheese remaining in my hand, poised above the grater.

"You've grated it *all*!" she exclaimed in disbelief at my extravagance. "At 200 rubles a kilo!" She shook her head, surprised by what must have seemed to her either a naive attitude about prices or a cavalier approach to money that only a Westerner, armed with dollars, could have. And indeed I had bought the cheese myself, for what amounted to little over a dollar but would have cost her almost one-fifth of her monthly salary as a musician.

The general mood of worry and pessimism I encountered during my three-week stay in Moscow is evident throughout the following narratives, based on conversations I had with the young people during my trip. For them, as for most people, the euphoria of glasnost is long over. In the face of rapid economic and social decline, interest in politics seems to have almost completely disappeared, despite the fact that the coup and the popular resistance that ended it remain a vivid and exciting memory for many—perhaps the last moment in which they felt enthusiastic about possibilities for change in the near future.

Much has changed in the lives of these young people during the three years since I last saw them. They have witnessed major social and political upheavals—an attempted military coup thwarted by mass demonstrations, the dissolution of the Soviet Union, increasingly violent interethnic strife, and a rapid decline in the standard of living of the majority of the population, their families included. Together with these momentous changes in their society, they have also experienced extremely important events in their personal lives—the loss of a parent; love, marriage, and the prospect of children; for some, graduation and entry into the world of work, for others the beginning of a higher education.

The fact that the young people are making important life decisions and experiencing significant personal changes at a moment of general national crisis probably accounts for the seriousness and feelings of responsibility expressed throughout these narratives. The young people voice their distress over the developments in their country and the difficulties people are experiencing, as well as an urgent need to "find oneself" in a society where there are no certain paths to the future. Most are also faced with the immediate challenge of earning enough money to help their parents or at least not to become an economic burden on them. While it is evident that traditional choices for career and work may no longer be viable, it is not clear what alternatives can replace them. One manifestation of uncertainty is the various attempts at commercial activity described by Alexei, Lyosha, and Dima, all of them beset by difficulties and obstacles, most resulting in failure. And for those who have entered an institution of higher education, once a step that guaranteed some type of job placement, it is not clear what kind of work, if any, will be available when they complete their studies, or whether that work will condemn them to a lifetime of low wages and a depressed standard of living, which Tanya expects to be her lot as a teacher. Even Ilya, who three years earlier was far more interested in discussing political events than his personal life, notes that now, with his wife experiencing a difficult pregnancy, the burden of housework has fallen on his shoulders and that he spends more time worrying about how to put a meal together than about social or political developments. The difficulty of coming of age at such a moment is expressed by Alexei, who told me, rather mournfully, "I'm living through a very complicated time period.

Terrible. I'm unlucky. Because before everything was simple and clear."

Yet throughout these conversations there is a feeling of energy and activity. And although the young people repeated to me on various occasions that they are no longer interested in politics, most of them continue to be acutely aware of current developments in their country's social and political life and display considerable emotion when discussing them.

The narratives that follow provide an update of the developments in the lives of a group of Moscow young people over the last three years. They also offer a view of life in post-Soviet Russia. Through their descriptions of their own lives and the lives of their friends and families, the young people reveal how some ordinary citizens are faring in this time of great change, crisis, and upheaval.

EDUCATION AND CAREER DECISIONS

When I left Moscow in 1989, the students about to graduate from vocational schools were facing urgent problems that required immediate resolution: for the boys, the obligation of military service, which most found undesirable, and for Olya, the prospect of a two-year obligatory work assignment in the factory where she had done her practicum, a prospect no more appealing to her than military service was for the boys. Almost all of the vocational school graduates went to considerable lengths to avoid those prospects. Of the boys, only Dima completed his full two years of military service—and he notes that he was almost the only one among his friends to have done so. Even Maxim, who three years earlier had seemed eager to serve in the military, also chose to obtain a false medical exemption when other young men challenged and tempted him to fool the army doctors. In a similar fashion, Olya escaped her undesired work assignment by obtaining a false medical certificate.

None of the vocational school graduates work in the trade for which he or she was trained, and none of them completed the required two-year work assignment that their vocational school arranged for them. Their vocational school training seems completely irrelevant for their lives after graduation. The first assignment given to Alexei by the vocational school (and from which he promptly fled) was a fruitless task of digging in a field for a lost telephone cable; the work had nothing to do with the carpentry skills he had studied. His experience illustrates the difficulties that vocational education has in making connections between school training and future work life. Only Dima, in a telephone conversation from Canada, where he is now living, told me that he has had any use for his training since graduation, repairing televisions and other appliances for acquaintances while living in Ontario. But even in this case, Dima's plans for the future do not involve the skills he acquired at the vocational school.

Finding work that is both fulfilling and can provide a decent income has been an immediate concern for the vocational-school graduates, none of whom see further schooling as a realistic possibility or one worth pursuing. Starting a small private business is one alternative they consider. Interestingly, at present this is an option considered *only* by the vocational-school students and, notably, only by the young men.

Lyosha, Alexei, and Dima have all become interested or involved in some form of entrepreneurial activity. While three years ago the possibility of practicing their trade in a cooperative seemed appealing, they are now more attracted by other new ways of "making money." Opening up a small business or joint enterprise, however, is a precarious undertaking. Many new businesses fold, and the difficulties of trying to run one are described by Alexei and Lyosha in considerable detail.

Olya is the only one of the vocational-school students who feels that these doors are not open to her. This is not surprising, given the increasing economic insecurity of women in

Russia today and the general exclusion of women from entrepreneurial pursuits. For Olya, the alternative to work in a factory production line is a low-paying clerical job.

Most vocational-school graduates, in retrospect, feel that
the choice to attend a vocational school was not a good one
and in essence has served to limit rather than broaden their
perspectives, despite new possibilities to open private businesses. However, they also question the usefulness of a
higher education. Olya notes that her colleagues are all
women with college degrees, yet they perform the same job
for the same salary as she does with her vocational-school
diploma.

Significantly, even those who finished the academic track,
were accepted into a college or university program, and are
currently engaged in studies have great doubts about the usefulness of a higher education and the wisdom of pursuing
one. Their doubts are due in part to the diminishing prestige
of higher education, a process accelerated by the intense criticism of the Soviet educational system during the period of
glasnost. In the Soviet system, a higher education was valued
and considered an important step for success and for integra-
tion into official society. With the demise of the old official
ideology, it is no longer of much relevance. Today economic
circumstances are influencing attitudes toward higher education, which no longer holds the promise of a job placement
or a successful career. A higher education is no longer necessary or even useful in gaining access to the most lucrative
types of activity, particularly the buying and reselling in
which so many people now engage. New, highly profitable
business opportunities are more attractive to many young
people than studies, even though such businesses are quite
unstable. As an example, Alexei's current success depends
upon the availability of eyeglass lenses hoarded from shipments of humanitarian aid, a supply that will run out sooner
or later. As Tanya points out, the most important distinction
in the future may not be between those with a higher educa-

tion and those without, but rather between those who work
for the shrinking and troubled state sector and those who
work independently in the more profitable private sector.

MARRIAGE AND THE CAREER
PROSPECTS OF WOMEN

Consistent with the trend among young people in the former
Soviet Union to marry and have children earlier than their
Western counterparts, there have been two marriages in the
three years since I left, and a third planned for the near
future. Both Natasha and Ilya, who have married friends they
met since 1989, will soon become parents. And Tanya, who
plans to marry soon, indicates that although she does not
want to become a parent in the near future, her fiancé is
already putting pressure on her to have a child.

Natasha's decision to stay at home with her child for five
years is in part attributable to the current changes: her father
and her husband have opened up their own construction
business and, thanks to the good connections and experience
of Natasha's father, their business is prospering. The 10,000
rubles per week that each of them was earning at the time of
my visit was a very large sum of money. In comparison, many
of the young people reported that their parents earned
between 1,500 and 2,500 rubles *per month*. If the family business continues to thrive, Natasha should have no particular
financial difficulties even if she does not work or study for
the next five years. Indeed, the salary she would earn as a primary-school teacher would add very little to the family's
material well-being.

Tanya's attitudes about marriage and career are also
important to note. Tanya remains committed to the idea of
working as a teacher and hopes that she will be able to find
work in her field, despite its low pay and prestige. However,
she is aware that by choosing to marry a man in the military,
she may be giving up the opportunity to work as a teacher

since she plans to follow her husband wherever his military assignment sends him, whether there is work for her there or not, and she notes that most military wives do not find work in their fields. She imagines her future as a cleaning woman, although just a few moments earlier, in the same conversation, she had proudly declared her commitment to the teaching profession regardless of the financial insecurity she anticipates.

Women in general occupy an increasingly precarious position in the labor market. They are often among the first to be laid off and make up 70–80 percent of the newly unemployed in Moscow. Public attitudes stereotype women as less capable of the risk taking and enterprise associated with opening a business, and women have a more difficult time than men securing the loans and financing to start one. In these conversations, there is frequent mention of the difficulties faced by mothers: Tanya, Alexei, and Katya discuss the problems their mothers have faced with layoffs and scant possibilities for other work. And it is probably no coincidence that the new businesses started by members of the young people's families involve only fathers. The fathers of Tanya, Yelena, and Natasha are all involved in private business. Although Alexei's mother is working on a free-lance basis, she is not attempting to open her own business; her status as a temporary worker is due not to choice but to the fact that she has been laid off from two jobs. Again, it is noteworthy that only the boys show interest in opening their own businesses. None of the girls even mention the possibility, except for Olya, who does so precisely to emphasize that for a "little Young Pioneer girl . . . straight from the vocational school," opening up a business is simply beyond the realm of the possible.

LIVING WITH ECONOMIC INSECURITY

Financial instability is a predominant theme in these narratives, as it is a predominant theme for everybody in Moscow.

Dramatic price increases and the hardship they have brought
to most people have had considerable impact on the young
people and on their thinking as they contemplate their passage into adulthood.

Financial independence seems to have become an unreach-
able goal. Lena, Yelena, Natasha, and Tanya seem resigned to
at least some degree of financial dependence on their parents for most of their adult lives. Ilya talks about the lack of
incentive for university students to engage in intellectual pursuits, citing the example of an acquaintance, a promising
Pasternak scholar, who is now involved in business—and, in
Ilya's opinion, "not the highest sort of business, either!"*
And Yelena says,

> In these times you have a choice: you either think about
> ways you can make money, get into business, or you think
> about spiritual, educational, not material things. One or
> the other. If you get 900 rubles a month for your work, you
> just decide you're going to live without a dacha† and with-
> out a car. Period.

The idea of living through adulthood in relative poverty
seems to be easier for the girls to accept than it is for the
boys, who for the most part are actively exploring ways to
earn more money. Their attitude may be explained by the
pressure that they, as males, feel to eventually become the

---

*In the interviews the young people used two terms for opening a busi-
ness or engaging in selling and reselling activities: *kommertsiia* and the Eng-
lish-borrowing *biznes*. Although they were used interchangeably, *biznes*
sometimes carries with it a greater touch of irony or criticism, perhaps
because its English origin symbolizes the Westernization of Russia, which is
controversial.

†Dachas are country homes commonly owned by urban families. For
ordinary families they are often quite simple, not more than a small house
or shack with a garden plot. The dacha provides an important opportunity
to leave the city on the weekend, breathe better air, and do gardening. It is
an increasingly important way for families to supplement their diet with
produce.

primary breadwinner and provider for their future families. Although throughout these narratives the boys express negative attitudes toward "speculation"—buying and then reselling for higher prices—it is equally evident that this type of commercial activity holds a certain temptation. Trips to Poland are mentioned with surprising frequency, and most often those trips are made for the purpose not of seeing Poland but of taking advantage of the commercial opportunities available there. Only Lena expresses pleasure about the trip she made to Poland as a tourist, and she describes with humor the behavior of her travel companions who spent their one day in Warsaw buying and selling rather than sight-seeing.

THE FUTURE

In 1989, at the beginning of this project, I was interested in learning to what degree the eleven teenagers felt empowered to determine what their lives would become. This question continued to concern me when I revisited them in 1992, three years later. It is clear that the general uncertainty and chaos engulfing post-Soviet society are affecting people's lives in many ways they cannot control. Old options are disappearing, but new opportunities are uncertain, making the current period an extremely confusing time for these young adults. They received most of their education and prepared themselves for the future under the old regime, but now find themselves facing an almost entirely new set of expectations about adult life and their role in society. The values and expectations about jobs, careers, and lifestyles that they inherited from the Soviet system have a much smaller place in the new Russia. Yet throughout these narratives, the young people assert that much of what happens to them depends on their efforts and how they prepare themselves for life. The entrepreneurial pursuits of Lyosha, Alexei, and Dima indicate a willingness to take advantage of new opportunities, just as Yelena's plans to take university entrance exams after three failures are evidence of her determination to take charge of her own future. Yet at the same time it is clear that the rapid changes have left many bewildered and unsure of what to do. As Tanya points out, in the new order, anyone who depends upon the old ways, anyone who remains an employee of the public sector—as she, a teacher, plans to do—will face lifelong difficulties.

Mixed in with worries, however, there is still a sense of curiosity and even excitement about what the future might bring. Several of the young people mentioned the possibility of doing another book in a few years, when, they say, there will be even more to talk about and report. But the current moment, with all its uncertainties, remains the primary preoccupation. Alexei described to me the way he has been thinking about our conversations during the last three years,

> I'm continuing the story I began to tell you then, I'm continuing the book.... Now some of my friends and I have been thinking that we should write a book called "Children of the Caves," about the children of these hungry times!

What happens to these young people will in great part be shaped by future developments in their country, Russia. The nature of these developments seems even less certain or predictable than it did three years ago, when I first met these young women and men as teenagers. New cohorts of sixteen- and seventeen-year-olds will undoubtedly be quite different from this generation, which has had, for better or worse, the experience of living through the end of adolescence during the first shock waves of one of the major political and social transitions of our times. Whether they will ultimately look back on themselves as the "children of perestroika," "children of the caves," "children of hungry times," or in terms of some other defining experience is yet to be determined.

"MARRYING FOR LOVE"

TANYA

*Nineteen years old, third-year student at
a teacher-training college*

*I meet Tanya in the metro station near her home. Her appearance
has changed very little: she still keeps her hair in a long braid and
has the same shy, lovely smile of three years ago, although she now
wears a touch of makeup. She links her arm through mine as we
climb the stairs of the station and begin talking.*

*This is the first time I have been inside Tanya's apartment. She
lives with her parents in two rooms with a kitchen and foyer. In the
kitchen a large chunk of meat, carefully protected by a piece of plas-
tic, lays defrosting in the sink for the evening meal. Peeled potatoes
soak in a pot of water on the counter. The apartment is clean and
bright and seems peaceful. Tanya tells me that she and her mother
share the large room, while her father, who likes to watch television
at night, inhabits the smaller one.*

*We sit at a table in the large room. Tanya has spent half of her
monthly student stipend to buy a meringue cake for the occasion,
and she serves it with tea and juice. The afternoon summer sun
heats the room through the open window, and the noise of Tanya's
busy street makes a taped interview difficult. She tells me that lately
there has been a lot of shooting at night near the metro station, and
she does not like to go outside after dark anymore.*

*A girlfriend stops by. She studies at Moscow's pedagogical uni-
versity and they want me to hear another perspective on the life of a
future teacher. The friend laughs. "A life of poverty!" she says. "But
we don't care," Tanya insists, with both pride and irony, as if*

15

TANYA

*laughing at her own naiveté and idealism. "We are going to teach
children!"*

*Later Tanya talks about Seryozha, her fiancé, in a calm, confi-
dent tone. She is certain that her marriage will be a good one. She
seems happy.*

The college where I study is sort of halfway between a
teacher-training school,* the kind that prepares people to
work in the first few grades of primary school, and an institute,† where one gets a higher education. They promised us a
diploma that will say "incomplete higher education," and they
built a new college, a new building. They told us that later on
we could finish our higher education at a pedagogical institute or university, but now nobody wants to accept us there!

My school is an experimental pedagogical college. This is
the third year that they are selecting a group of students.
Before there were only pedagogical schools, which students
entered after the ninth grade for three years of training to
teach primary school. In my college, the students enroll after
completing eleventh grade, for a three-year program. The
good thing about the college is that they demand a lot of
practical work with schoolchildren. For a year and a half we
went to schools, played with the kids, organized holiday parties for them, and now for a whole year we'll be teaching.
First we'll have some practice lessons, and then for three

---

*The schools that have traditionally prepared primary-school teachers
are not part of the system of higher education. Students, mainly young
women, enter these schools upon completion of the ninth grade, thus leaving the academic track and receiving a technical education. Tanya's college
represents an attempt to raise the quality and prestige of teacher-training
programs.

†There are several words used throughout these narratives that refer to
institutions of postsecondary education. "Institute" in Russian generally
refers to an institution of higher education other than a university. However, "institutes" and universities both fit within the general category of
"institution of higher education," commonly referred to by the Russian
acronym, VUZ *(vysshee uchebnoe zavedenie)*.

months at the end of the year we'll work full-time in a school. At our college they really emphasize practice, whereas at an institute they spend more effort on theory. And that's why they don't want to accept us at an institute to finish our higher education! We already know how to do everything. That's why they say to us, good, all of you, go ahead, keep thinking about finishing your higher education, but for now, just get out there and look for work. And it's hard to find work in schools now.

I don't know in what sense you could really call the college experimental. I think things are basically the way they always were. Most of our classes have to do with teaching methodology—teaching math, teaching Russian language, reading, many things. And then there is this "new" subject, history of the fatherland, where we're going over everything for the twenty-fifth time, there's absolutely nothing new there at all. Our teacher reads lectures and she seems very cautious, doesn't tread on any new ground. Of course I understand it's a very controversial question. Even at the university, in the history department, I understand their position is, "You're already grown-ups, intelligent, read about history yourselves." We're just listening to those same old lectures . . . and we don't have any new textbooks. There's a trial textbook, *History of the Fatherland*. It's two volumes, an anthology. But look, even there, anytime there's anything written about Lenin—I've seen this personally now at least four times—they write about him as the best, the most original, the most capable. But the director of our school did tell us that when that book came out, a lot of people, a lot of historians, really criticized it for not being very objective. But I have to say that lots of what's in that book are things that we already heard three years ago, in grade school, from our history teacher, Warshavsky.*

---

*In Tanya's secondary school, students felt that this young and very unconventional history teacher was one of the major signs that glasnost had indeed appeared at their school.

By the way, he's still teaching there. But from what I've heard, nobody at school listens to him. They don't care. It's not interesting to the kids. We were really interested in it then! Because we were hearing those things from Warshavsky just after we had finished reading completely different things in the old textbooks. What he talked about was really something else—all those figures, the numbers of people murdered, the number of people who died from hunger, all those things simply shocked us. I've been hearing that the students who are there now are very different from the way we were. I remember how people used to go around saying, about us, "Oh, those young people. They don't care about anything." But that wasn't true. We did care! But now, the students at that school, of course you can't say that they're bad, but they've all gone in only one direction—into commerce! Of course those students who are going into commerce are more optimistic than I am! When you've got some money in your pocket, it's easier to be optimistic. So maybe something will come of those students after all.

At the college we had a practicum, but they had us running around, from school to school. Half a year here, half a year there. You get used to the kids at one place, then it's on to the next. It's useful to see how a teacher plans a lesson, all those purely methodological questions. But then you see how the teachers relate to the kids, how they really don't care about anything, about the kids. They have an attitude like, "What are you kids doing over there? Well, do what you want, as long as you're not breaking each other's heads!" So of course I didn't really enjoy the practicum. In one school we talked with the administration; it was just an ordinary school, with no specialization, but you would have thought from what they said that the school was really excellent, really something else, and that the kids were so smart. But once you've seen that school, you realize what they said was such nonsense. And I've noticed that parents often have very bad feelings toward the schools, too. I think they fooled us when

we decided to enter this college. They told us it would be like
an institute, that we were part of something really special,
but in reality they palmed off a bunch of mediocre teachers
on us. We feel that even though we've only studied for two
years, we already know a lot more than some of the old teachers we've observed in schools. When you're a new, young
teacher, and you go to work in a school, the administration
looks at you as if . . . well, there are no real opportunities for
new teachers. Only if you go, as one of our teachers advised
us, to the new innovative schools, like Shatalov's, or
Amonashvili's,* that's the only place you'll really get to teach.
In ordinary schools things are so sad. But my plans are still
firm. No matter what, I'm still going to teach.

This summer I was getting ready to go on a practicum, to
work at a pioneer camp, and I was a little apprehensive. I
didn't know what I was going to do with those kids for thirty-
five days! I was thinking of games, collecting some materials
to bring. But now I just found out that we're not going. One
session in a pioneer camp now costs 15,000 rubles, and it's
gotten too expensive for the parents to send their kids. So
they're going to have only a few groups, not nearly as many
as they had planned originally, and so they called the college
and said they were no longer interested in hiring us. They
don't have the money to pay us! Imagine, at that camp, thirty-five days, 10–15,000 rubles a kid! And I remember my
mother paid 67 rubles for me for twenty-four days. That was
expensive, too, for those days, but we only paid a third of it
because the trade union paid the rest. But I remember last
summer things had already gotten expensive. Going to a
camp cost 800 rubles,† and most kids simply stayed in
Moscow for the summer. And there were a lot of accidents,

---

*Contemporary educators known and respected for their innovative
approaches. See Shalva A. Amonashvili, *Hello, Children! A Teacher's Guide*,
translated in *Soviet Education*, vol. 30, nos. 4, 5 (April–May 1988).

†Prices are a common and important topic throughout these narratives.
The reader should keep in mind that, while there had been price increases

lots of kids got hurt, children got run over. They're trying to keep that from happening again. I remember they were talking about thousands of accidents, hundreds of deaths.

In any case, the college administration is talking about setting something up where we go to a day camp in the city, for a month, without getting any pay for it, so we get the practice.

There was a strike of kindergarten teachers because the price of food went up so much. The kids' parents weren't able to pay for food either. The teachers demanded a pay increase. Imagine, they are paid even less than primary-school teachers. They're mainly women, probably more than half of them don't have a higher education, and so of course they get paid very little. And so they went on strike and made demands for a long time, and now a bunch of kindergartens are going to be closed for lack of funds. So the strikes didn't change a thing. Parents are in such a state. They have to go to work, and they've got little kids, and anyone who doesn't have an alternative—if, for example, there's no grandmother in the family. . . . That's why when Natasha* has her child, I don't know. I ask her, "Natasha, what are you going to do?" She's going to have a hard time. And it's gotten so expensive to give birth. About 2,000 rubles. Everybody says that the birthrate has really fallen in Moscow. But of course Natasha and her family are in a good situation. She's going to depend a lot on her father, as the head of the family. He earns a lot of money since he started his own business. So they're going to live off their parents' backs. And they're going to live like that for a long time because it takes a lot of money to feed a little kid!

---

and general inflation before January 1992, after the breakup of the Soviet Union and the introduction of new economic policies by the Yeltsin government, price increases became extremely steep. The month of January 1992 thus has particular significance in these discussions and is often the reference point in comparisons of prices "then" and "now."

*Natasha (also interviewed in this book) and Tanya studied at the same secondary school and entered the experimental college at the same time.

Mom says to me, "I won't be able to help you and Seryozha at all! I simply won't be able to!" And I say, "Mom, that's okay, don't worry."

PARENTS' LIVES

Mom moved into another office at the same place where she was working. She's earning more because she's gone to a full-time schedule. I don't really know what she does, she just sits like before, in some stuffy office. But she's earning more, since she used to work half-time. She earns 1,500 rubles a month. She still doesn't really like her job, but at least there's a lot of people in her office now, a lot of women, so they all come to work, it's a good atmosphere, they get to talking. Before she just worked with one other person. They would just sit there and get on each other's nerves.

Dad's doing just what he was before, too, except that now he and about ten other people, all of whom are electricians, like Dad, have opened up a small joint enterprise. They joke about how soon they'll go to America, build some things over there! He's feeling pretty good because, after all, they pay him well. Now there's a stimulus to do some work, because they get paid a lot. He gets about 3,500–4,500 a month. That's a good wage. Look, a teacher gets 1,300, 1,200, sometimes only 900! And before the electricians used to have to bow down to some boss there, do what he said, but now they tell the boss, "Look, we'll fulfill all the work we have to do to complete the Plan, but in addition we'll add whatever jobs we want." For example, they'll do the wiring for some store, but of course not during their working hours. It used to be that they looked down on moonlighting, but now it's become official, legal, and they have their own little group there, called Elektrika. They work a lot more. They used to do two or three stores a day. Now, he says, "I go wherever I'm invited to work." Everybody who works at Elektrika divides up the money they make.

So the changes in this society have helped Dad, but my mom, well, I don't know. She's still just sitting there in an office from nine to six. It's boring. Then she still has to go shopping, bring something home to eat, and everything's gotten so expensive here now. The only thing she says that's good about her job is that it's only half an hour from home, and she's working with people she knows and likes. Her people. She works at a military school where they train border guards. I suppose it's not a very reliable place to work right now! If they cut back on the military, they'll keep giving my mother and her colleagues the hope that they will transfer them to some other workplace. And really, they could cut back on the military at any moment. She already faced the threat of being laid off once. But she's been working there for a long time. They suggested transferring her someplace else, downtown, on Dzerzhinsky, but the place was really bad, full of cockroaches, no colleagues, good pay but bad conditions. So she prefers to stay where she is as long as she can.

My parents are offended by what's going on. The same way they lived with the old prices, they're measuring by the old yardstick. There really is a sense of disillusionment in them. Dad says, "Look, we lived in communism," and I say, "Dad, when?" And then he says, "I remember how I used to live in the 1960s and the early 1970s. I remember all that and I'm going to tell my grandchildren how it was, how we lived in communism." Of course he's very dissatisfied with everything now. He watches *Vremya** on television now and compares the way things were. My parents were hoping things would get better, but they think things have gotten worse. They were full of hope about Gorbachev, then about Yeltsin, but now they've started calling Yeltsin *Borka,* "Little Boris," and I can see that Yeltsin's authority has obviously fallen, once they've started calling him that!

My optimism has really fallen, too. I wouldn't say it's disap-

---

*The evening news program.

peared, but it's dropped quite a bit. Because I don't know if
I'm going to get a job, even though everywhere you look
there aren't enough teachers. And of course my student
stipend, 285 rubles, doesn't make me very happy! I can't even
buy myself a cake with my stipend! If I buy myself one cake,
with my monthly stipend, I'm left with 200 rubles for the
month, and what does that leave me, 10 rubles a day? And
bread costs 7 rubles a loaf.* So, as they say around here now,
think about the worst, but hope for the best! Everybody's joking now, Wait, wait! Our grandchildren will live under communism. Maybe we'll build it one of these days. The girls at
college joke like this. But that word "communism" is a word
that's empty, that has no meaning. Of course Dad thinks we
used to live under communism, that if we measure the way
we used to live, in those times, everything was great. But I
don't argue with him. He remembers how a half-liter bottle
of vodka used to cost 24 rubles, and now it costs 100, 150! A
crazy price! And bread, that used to cost 14 kopecks a loaf.
So he thinks that all we have to do is change our prices back
to those pennies and that's it, we'll have communism. That's
what my father says.

My parents are getting through one day at a time. They
won't lay off my father, but they might lay off my mother if
they want. They might pay the monthly salary, or they might
not. This winter we went for four months without getting
paid any money at all! They just didn't pay salaries. Of course
we didn't go hungry during the winter, we just didn't have
any money. We ate what we already had—the meat we had in
the freezer. We ate macaroni, even though we're used to potatoes, but they are too expensive. We didn't have the money.

All these reforms are being carried out at our expense, as
usual. The leadership doesn't want to think about how to

---

*As an example of the rapid inflation referred to in these narratives, by
the time I left Moscow two weeks later, the price had already gone up to
11–14 rubles a loaf.

help people. But how can the government carry out reforms at the expense of people who work for eight hours a day at the factory and have big families? Things are so bad around here that everybody really feels terrible. My cousin came here once, to Moscow. She had hurt her head in a fall, and she had to come and get an operation, and she went to a surgeon here. They sent her to a special hospital here for neurological illnesses, and she said there were so many sick women there, all sick with nervous stress, all those psychological illnesses. People just weren't like this before! People are simply getting sick standing in these lines, they're all over each other, they get so angry. It's not possible to live like this! I suppose some people are making it. There is a certain sector that's living all right, that doesn't have to worry about the problem of how to go on living. There is that class of people here now. And in general the division of classes is going to go to levels no one would have thought of before.

The ideology has changed. It used to be that being a worker was considered something to be proud of, even if those were just empty words. Now that's changed. And even if working-class people really do get the chance to *work*, people are still going to view the working class as something dirty, unwashed. The difference between the classes is going to get greater and much harder to cross.

People discuss everything, but nobody's doing anything. Maybe people are too tired. After all, what is this now, the fifth year of changes? Nobody wants to work, they all want to go into commerce. After all, everybody is sick and tired of hearing what they've been promising us. Even those who are still working, they also get promised that "we'll pay you for what you do." But they don't get paid! That's why it seems to me that doing manual labor now is really bad, especially for those who work in industry. The only good thing now is that they've allowed people to start their own joint enterprises and get stockholders. Those people work and get their money. But for those who work at a government enterprise—

as a teacher I'm in that position, I depend entirely on government money—our work doesn't pay for itself because we don't produce anything. That's why whatever the government is able to pay us, that's what they pay us. But what about when they don't want to anymore, or can't? And we get less than everybody. Medical workers, cultural workers, and teachers—the poorest, the most miserable. Working for the public sector means having a life of financial problems. Even so, that's what I want to do: I want to teach. I am going to teach children! But teachers, doctors, anybody who works for the public sector is not going to have an easy time in life, and I know I am creating problems for myself by making the choice that I am making.

There are private schools now, but they say it's very hard to get work in one of them because there are very few of them and the competition is really tough. Actually there's even a religious school now; it goes up to the tenth grade. One of our college teachers sends her daughter to that religious school. And that girl is enchanted with the school. Our teacher says, "Listen, don't even think of sending your kids anywhere else but to a school like that!" Of course I'd like to work in a school like that, but I think it would be very difficult to find a job there. I'm really worried about where I'll find work. I only have one more year left to study, and then it will be time to go to work.

SERYOZHA

Seryozha, my future husband, is studying at a military school. He's going to be a soldier. He studies at the same place Mom works; that's how we met. Actually he's my second young man. The first was also a future soldier, but from the academy. We were together for a year. That was so useless, a real waste of time! It's really true what they say, "Where the army begins, all order stops." All his concentration went into his strength, his muscles. Of course, he did have some interest in technical things, too, but he really he wasn't interested in anything else. A year wasted. I really regret it. I just didn't know how else to go about things. He was my first boyfriend, after all. Once I met a friend of his, another soldier, and I liked him better. He was really at a higher level. But of course, to him I was already a lost cause! I was his friend's girlfriend!

Seryozha is really a kind person. A fountain of kindness! He's not very handsome. You couldn't even call him attractive. And compared to my first boyfriend, well my father used to say that my first boyfriend was simply an Apollo! So good-looking! But the second one is simply a good person. Actually my girlfriends, when they first saw him, said to me sort of quietly, "Good lord, what in the world have you dug up for yourself?" But after we started hanging around together, going to birthday parties as a group, they all started saying that he really is a good person. He relates to others as if they were, well, if not relatives, then close friends. The only problem he has is that he's really nervous. His commander is a big shot and has been on his back for four years. So Seryozha can get pretty nervous from all those orders in the army. But his good qualities compensate for that.

Seryozha is twenty-two. He started his studies late because he served in the army first. See, his father is in the military and so is his brother, and so he thought, "All right, I'm not going to walk away from you guys, I'll go into the army as well." But I don't really think he wanted to go into the army, to be a soldier. He studies there because he promised his father he would. His father got very ill, and he asked Seryozha, "Will you study in the military school?" And Seryozha promised him that he would. About a half-year after that his father died. So as it turned out, he really must study there because he gave his word. But his desire to study there was really pretty weak. I don't know if he'd rather do something else, but I think so, maybe repairing cars. He knows mechanics very well, and sometimes he says that it would be better if he could work with his hands. He thinks he's wasting his time in that school; he doesn't like what they teach them there at all.

Seryozha's brother studied at the military school, too, four years, and he says he lost four years of his life. For the most part the commanders there are a bunch of old men, and you can feel how tough they are, you know, close to the KGB and all that.

If Seryozha were to leave the military as soon as he finished his studies, he could become a teacher of the military preparedness course we have in schools here. He has the training to become a teacher. Or he could become a teacher of physical education, in any school or institute. Actually, right now a lot of men who have finished military schools are organizing their own businesses, working as security guards. That's something they know how to do well! But Seryozha doesn't want to. He doesn't want to go around with a weapon. He says, "I don't like the idea that just to protect somebody else's possessions I could end up paying with my health or with my life." Especially if he has a family, he really doesn't want to take that risk. So he's getting ready to serve as a border guard in the army as soon as he finishes his schooling. I think the service is twenty-five years until retirement. And he has already served four years. So there's only a little bit of time left—twenty-one years!—until he can collect his pension.

After they finish their studies at his school, they're posted throughout the territory of the former Soviet Union, the Commonwealth of Independent States. They send a lot of people to the Caucasus or to Central Asia, but he says, "No, I won't go there." His father spent his whole life serving at the farthest end of the Soviet Union! In Central Asia. He remembers how bad the water was, the food, the unbearable heat, and how everything spoils.

His future is uncertain. After all, he's a border guard! So he's watching what's going on very carefully. He'll get work in any event, but perhaps they'll send him to the Far East or

Central Asia, and I'll have to go with him. The only good thing about it is that they'll pay him a lot more if he goes there, instead of, let's say, the Finnish border, or the western border. They'll pay better there because we'll be living worse! His brother ended up in Central Asia, and he knows just how things are there. Completely uncivilized small ethnic groups, although I suppose the Turkmens, who also live there, are considered a large nationality group. But it's so wild there on the border that you can't even describe it! There is no civilization there at all. They don't speak or understand Russian. They think that everything in Moscow is Moscow, but everything on the border is theirs, and they refuse to live in any other way. You can't explain anything to them! Seryozha says that they just cross over the border freely, just like that, and when you say something, they reply, "So what? That's our native Mongolia over there, our native China! Those are our brothers, everywhere!"

I don't find the idea of living there, in another culture, interesting. I'd rather go to the Baltic region, or even to the Far East. But that Central Asian region, the guys who have served there, well, they come back so tired, so indifferent, and the ones with families come back with a head full of gray hair! It's bearable for those who don't have families, but really, even the words "Central Asia" scare people! It's the end! Maybe not the end of your career, but the end of your strength, the end of your health. He really doesn't want to go there. But if we get married, I'll have to go there with him. And I won't find any work there. I've already started thinking about this. Perhaps I should take some courses, basic medical care, accounting, perhaps, how to do paperwork. I have to get used to the idea that I might end up with a specialization completely different from the one I am training for. But it won't be for a long time. He's promised that he'll do everything possible to make sure we won't go there for long. Look, his mother lived there her whole married life, and she's from Russia. She left her health behind in Central Asia. I don't

know how she raised three children there, it was such a hard
life. She really wasn't thrilled when she saw how her husband
was persuading his sons to go into the military, too, to
become border guards. After all, she did that her whole life,
and she suffered.

BEING A MILITARY WIFE

It doesn't make any difference to me that the Soviet Union
doesn't exist anymore. It hasn't really touched my life in any
way. But for soldiers its been really bad. I know that when we
had elections for the presidency of Russia, General Makashov was a candidate, and for the most part military people
voted either for him or for Ryzhkov because they were for the
preservation of the Union.* And since now there is no Union
and no all-Union army, there's no place to live, especially for
those who have been pulled out of the GDR, or from Hungary. They brought those soldiers back and they all have
three kids and old parents here in Russia who are not in a
position to take them in to live. And so a lot of them are living in tents. Of course for the guys with all the stars on their
chests it's not so awful. But the lieutenants and the lower-
ranking people, they're all living in barracks with terrible
conditions. It used to be prestigious to be in the army. There
was always work and it was pretty well paid, too.

Of course I joke to Seryozha, "There's no incentive for me
to marry you!" But of course I'm marrying for love. It used to
be the case that these military schools were popular. There
were always lots of girls hanging around them. It was considered prestigious to marry a soldier or a border guard. Now
one could only marry a soldier for love, because there are no
advantages whatsoever. A sensible girl wouldn't go after a

---

*General Albert Makashov would be dismissed from the army in 1991
because of his involvement in the August coup. He later played a central
role in the violent events of October 1993. Nikolai Ryzhkov was the Soviet
prime minister under Gorbachev.

military man at all! I suppose if the husband is a good one
somehow you'll do okay, you won't notice that your whole life
is spent out of suitcases. But if things don't go well in the
family, imagine. For some reason military men have a lot of
kids. It must be because they're gone all the time, all those
trips, and then they come home and you know, right away,
such love! And right away—children! But I think that there is
a desire on the part of wives to get divorced. For at least the
first ten years of marriage the wife thinks about that. They
want to get out of there, to wherever! That's the way Seryozha's brother got divorced from his wife. He came home
one day and found an empty apartment with a note, "Forgive
me, but I can't go on like this anymore." She couldn't take it.
And it happens like that a lot. He's got a second wife now, a
really great woman. But women are all very different.

I have a girlfriend who married a military man. He's in
Alma-Ata now, studying, and she's in a bit of shock because
she got pregnant. And he still has a year to finish studying,
and she keeps saying, "I don't know where we're going to end
up being sent, and imagine, with a little kid!" She'll probably
stay here in Moscow a year until he's finished, and then she'll
join him, but she'll leave the baby in Moscow with its grandmother. And then she'll come back for the child. But for now
they don't know where they're going, where they'll live. She's
hanging in there, trying to be cheerful about it, but . . . Of
course there are people who have a lot of *blat** who manage
to find a way to stay in Moscow, but those who don't, well,
they go wherever the motherland sends them.

I'll be here in Moscow two more years, preparing myself.
When Seryozha first came to ask for my hand—that's the tradition here—well, even though my mother had already understood that it was going to end up in a wedding, she started to
cry and said, "I just don't want to let you go anywhere! I

---

*A common slang word referring to various types of connections a per-
son may use to obtain consumer goods in scarce supply, services, or special
privileges.

didn't raise you to have you go off so far and live like that!" I told her, "But I'm already grown up," and she said, "Of course you are." After all, I'll be twenty-two then. Naturally, for my mother this is all very difficult. I tell her that it's not that I want to go! I think she was hoping that I would have a series of boyfriends first, she wasn't ready for me to marry, but from Seryozha's side it was serious from the very beginning, immediately. We had only known each other three months when he came here and proposed. For my mother it was a shock. After all, the women she works with, they're all the wives of military men, every second one has completed a higher education, and they've been working all their lives in any place you can imagine except in the profession they trained for! Some of them have worked as cleaning ladies, some cleaning streets, and they're really well-educated women! They've had to do such dirty work, and they look so tired!

I say to my mother, "But one has to love, right?" And I say to Seryozha, "I'm giving up everything for you, I'll follow you anywhere, Seryozha!" I guess I don't really know yet what it will mean to pick up and go someplace else. Maybe by the time you come back to Moscow I won't even be here anymore! But don't worry, if you come back to Moscow I'll be able to come here for a week because my work won't be very important there, so I'll be able to leave it. If I were a teacher, of course, I'd have a study program, responsibilities, but if I end up working as a cleaning lady. . . .

The military is hard for wives. If the wife of a general shows up that's one thing, but if a young lieutenant comes with a young wife, no matter what, even if she goes to the library and says, "You have to give me work here, after all, I've finished the university," so what? They'll still put a rag in her hands! And they'll send her to the library, all right—to clean it!

But that's because we have such a system. The government cares but not enough. Seryozha saw a kind of poll where they were asking about which careers were most prestigious, and the army was in the twelfth spot. And there were only about fifteen professions on the list!

MARRIAGE

I don't want to have children right away. But of course a husband wants to be a father right away, he wants to feel that. I tell Seryozha, "No, you'll have to wait a bit to become a father," but he acts like he has this unbearable desire to have a child. But perhaps it's also because there are some advantages in getting a work assignment with a child. He has two years left to finish studying, and if his child were already one and a half, he could get some advantages in his posting.

But it also depends upon whether I finish my higher education or go to work. Of course, I can have a child and stay at home with it, up to five years now, they say, although all they'll give you is 200 rubles a month to do that. Fine, stay at home and get 200 rubles a month! It's gotten so complicated to have a child, so expensive. My friend who's pregnant now is really in a state of shock over this. She tells me she doesn't know what to do. Our free medicine is in such bad shape, but to pay a doctor is so expensive! On the other hand, the girls who want to do it go ahead and do it. Already three girls who graduated with me from tenth grade have had children or are pregnant. My mother says, "Of course I want a grandchild, but I'm still young for that!" She's forty-five.

And a wedding costs so much now! It used to cost 1,000, and now it costs 30,000, 40,000! Who knows how much it will cost by next year! And Seryozha's family won't even be able to come in from the Far East, because the airline tickets are too expensive.

His relatives say, "Don't worry, you'll manage, you're grown-ups!" So I say to him, "Seryozha, I don't want to live off my parents, so tell me, how are we going to manage?" Because when you work for the state sector now, as we are going to, it means that you will never become self-sufficient.

It forces you to be dependent. The only people who are independent are the few people who manage to get involved in business on the side. I think even Seryozha did this, because when I first met him, he had a lot of money. But then he gave up his business because he doesn't have time to do anything else at the moment, and now he hardly has any money at all. We used to go to McDonald's to eat. We paid a lot of money and ate very little! We like McDonald's around here, it's kind of exotic. But after a while he let me know that he's not involved in business any longer because he was spending all his free time with me. So I said, "That's okay, I won't ask you for anything else. We'll just be poor students together!"

"STILL A WORKER"

OLYA

Twenty years old, office worker

Olya and her mother, Diana Nikolayevna, have invited me to have lunch at their home. Olya meets me at the metro station. She is a little late and rushes up to me, breathless. She has grown heavier in the last three years, and is wearing a pair of extremely high heels that make her look much taller than I remember. We hug and then leave the station together, at the same quick pace. We wait for a bus to take us to her building.

Olya asks me many questions about my life during the last three years, almost too quickly for me to answer. We are close to her building before I can begin to ask her questions about her life. As we enter the lobby of the building she tells me that she is the only one of her girlfriends who has not yet married, and, just short of twenty-one, she worries that she is becoming an old maid. I don't have time to ask her about any boyfriends before we leave the elevator and enter her apartment, but once we are inside, the story becomes clearer. The phone rings. Olya answers and immediately becomes agitated. Phone in hand, she paces the floor and, after listening for a few moments, says abruptly, "Well, I haven't heard from you in weeks and now you decide to appear?" There is silence and then Olya speaks again. "You don't need to bother calling me anymore." She hangs up the phone and is obviously upset. I look at her and she laughs a little in spite of her worry. "I'll tell you everything," she promises, and goes into the kitchen to greet her mother and announce our arrival.

Later we sit at the table for a meal that is simple but has obvious-

35

OLYA

ly taken Olya and Diana Nikolayevna considerable cost and effort to produce; many of the items are expensive and difficult to find in the stores. There is milk, sausage, and cheese, fried potatoes, and a salad of fresh cucumber and tomato with sour cream. There is also vodka and wine. I learn that Olya's father still has not left the apartment and that the four members of the family occupy the same two rooms they did three years ago. "And he'll never leave," Diana Nikolayevna says in disgust. She seems tired and older than I remember, but Olya later tells me that her mother has just worked the night shift and has not slept in two days.

They tell me that they cannot take advantage of one of the new government programs to create private ownership by buying their state-owned apartment, even though the price is not expensive. The apartment is in Olya's father's name, and if they privatized it, it would belong to him, and the family would then be taken off the list to receive government housing when a larger apartment becomes available.

As we eat, Diana Nikolayevna pours a shot of vodka for each of us. With her glass raised in the air, she proposes a toast: "Well, are we going to execute all men, or what?" Olya laughs and moves her glass toward her mother's. Seeing my moment's hesitation to join in this toast, Diana Nikolayevna gives me a sharp, scrutinizing look from across the table. "Nu nu," she says, her glass still raised, "she went off and got married and now she's taking it all back." She doesn't smile, but Olya laughs. I do too, and say, "Don't worry, I haven't become a traitor to my gender!" With this Diana Nikolayevna laughs, too, but there is a bitterness in her voice I had not heard during our meetings three years ago.

At the end of June [1989] we defended our diplomas at the PTU* and they started giving us work assignments. I was assigned to the polygraphic factory Gosznaka, where I had my practicum. Of course nobody wanted to go there to work,

---

*The Russian acronym for a vocational school (*politekhniche-skoe uchilishche*).

especially the girls. But we were supposed to work there for
two years, so we started to talk about how we could get out of
it. It was easier for the boys because they were on their way to
the army. But there were five of us girls who were supposed
to stay there to work. So one of my girlfriends said to me,
"Listen, Olya, my vision is bad, I'm going to get a medical
certificate that says I can't work there for health reasons."
And she was able to get one easily because the truth is that
they really were about to do an operation on her at the Fyo-
dorov eye clinic. So she got her medical certificate, and it
wasn't a trick. A second girl got married and so she went off
on maternity leave. Of course she wasn't planning on working there! There were three girls left. Another girl I had gotten to know said to me, "Look Olya, I have an acquaintance
who is a doctor, let's get a medical certificate that says we
can't work there." And so I got a medical certificate that said
I couldn't work there, couldn't work at any polygraphic factory, because I was allergic to some of the chemicals they use
there. I got out of it. But really they weren't too anxious to
take me at the factory anyway, because I didn't work there
very hard, especially during the last part of the practicum; I
just didn't want to work at all. The whole time I knew that
even if they wanted to take me there to work, there was no
way I was going to. Somehow or another I was going to get
out of there. As it turned out I got the certificate. I was
released!

That whole summer I stayed at home. I even was able to go
on a little vacation and rest a bit. And then I went with a girlfriend of mine to the Vnukovo airport to work. We wanted to
become stewardesses. We started to work there in the kitchen
for a while. Flying is one thing—it sounds romantic, the pilots
and all—but of course cleaning potatoes and that kind of work
is another thing! We had to work in the kitchen because the
people who are in charge there are really idiots. They think
that if a girl wants to work on a plane she needs to go through

some sort of preparatory phase. So a person who wants to work flights has to go through that kitchen work at the airport. But I don't think that assignment has anything to do with the work! I think they just send people wherever they need somebody to fill jobs at the airport, wherever they are short of hands, as if it were training. And so when a person wants to work on the planes, they say, "Well, you know, we do happen to have an open slot for you." And then they use people who are supposed to be going through flight training to work in the kitchen until they can find a permanent worker! And they promise that you'll get to fly that way. It's such an idiotic way of doing things! They say, "If you work for eight months in the kitchen, we'll take you as a member of the flight crew!" But they just have you there all those months because they need a worker to fill that position, and they don't have anybody. Nobody wants to take those kinds of jobs!

I only worked there about ten days. Then I left. I never did get to fly. It was too hard in that kitchen. In the first place, it was really far from my house and it took a long time to get there, and in the second place it was hard work, at night, so you didn't get to sleep at night. Very, very hard. And our hands of course were a real mess, all full of cuts and nicks, unpainted nails, dirty. It was really terrible. So I left that job. My girlfriend stayed in the kitchen though, worked her eight months, and then she did get to fly. But by that time I didn't want that job anyhow, I wasn't interested in flights, airplanes. None of that was for me.

That was in November. Around the end of February I went to work in an agency, the Moscow Transportation Agency, on Leninsky Prospekt. Even though their positions were filled they told me to come back in a week because one girl was getting ready to go out on maternity leave. So I went back there in a week, and I started working on the third of March. A whole year went by so fast, just flew by! The only difficult thing was that it's hard to work in the summer. I was used to spending my summers on vacation someplace, relaxing.

Then I took a vacation at the end of May, beginning of June, two weeks, I went to the south to rest. I came back and got to work again. Work, work, work. Of course there was a lot of work at first, and I thought I couldn't handle it. But then I got used to it, because in the first place I work with people there, and I get along with people. It's personal contact. And then of course I have changed, or life has changed, something changed. Look, if you're working in a factory, printing things, that's one thing, but if you work with people, well, everyone you work with is different, every new customer has something unique. You can't imagine the kind of people who show up there! You just end up sitting there, staring at them! They're all so different. You see, every person shows up there with his own life story, his own fate, his own mood, his own constitution. If somebody shows up in a bad mood, it ruins *your* day and *your* mood, too. Say that person's been in a store waiting in line, and the place really got on his nerves, and he's cross, what am I going to do, stand there smiling in his face?

I receive the orders for transporting shipments to various depots in Moscow. We also send containers outside of Moscow, but my job is to deal only with the ones that come into Moscow. For example, I arrange the containers that come from Brest, from Poland, for the most part from the socialist countries. The containers arrive at the station, the station sends us the information, we send a telegram to the address of the place that is supposed to receive the container, they pay us money and then we get the container to them. For the most part we deal with shipments for private individuals, not with many companies. We deal with small containers, and companies send large containers, twenty-ton containers. We transport things like furniture, household goods, those kinds of things that are sent to other cities. What we get for the most part are the things sent by people who work in the military academies. We get things from military people every day of the year. After they finish the military academy, the families are sent to other cities. So they send things. But actually we're getting fewer people now because the military academies are disintegrating little by little, and there are fewer people in them. And there are going to be even fewer because I've heard that people are going to have to start paying for their studies there, especially if they're going abroad, now that there is no Union anymore. And not just anybody can pay that kind of money to study. So I think we're going to have less work in the future because of what's happening in the military.

Our agency is the Moscow Transportation Agency, but actually we've formed a small cooperative there and we really just rent space from the agency. At first we were part of a state enterprise. But after that they turned us into a cooperative.* The director, Alexei Alexeyevich, is a really kindhearted man, a very soft person. I like the work a lot. In the first place, I only work every other day. It's hard to work every day. You really have to get used to it. But working every other day, well let's say I get up today at six o'clock, and go to work at eight, then by eight o'clock I'm free, I come home, and the next day I have the whole time free. So I can sleep in, go out for a walk, go someplace to visit a friend, take care of errands, the whole day is completely free. So my work is really convenient.

My salary is only 1,000 rubles. Of course I can't live off that money, not with the prices we have today. In order to live, to dress, to eat, minimally, it's hard to say what I need. Every month my expenses are so different. For example, this month I spent only for food, but some other month in addition to food I might need to buy some clothing. And so I won't have any money left at all that month. I might have completely unexpected purchases. I might end up spending

---

*Please see the glossary for clarification of this term.

3,000 in one day, or I might end up spending no more than 2,000 in a whole month. So that's why it's hard to say how much I need. But of course, the more money the better!

I buy food for the house. I buy what I find in the stores, what looks good to me, for everybody at home. Tomatoes, cucumbers, sausages, whatever I find, no matter how much it costs I buy, because I know we have to have vitamins in our diet. I spend about 500 rubles a month on food and I have the rest for other things. But I can do that because my mother feeds me. My mother buys most of the food for the house. I buy some things, but she buys the most. So I can spend the remaining 500 rubles on other things. But of course if your salary is 1,000 rubles and you want to buy a pair of shoes that cost 2,500—well, somehow we manage to buy them. Somehow we manage to shoe ourselves, clothe ourselves.

I'm still a worker, I don't deny that. I'm from a working family. I'd never turn my back on that and say that I'm from a family of the intelligentsia. I chose to work in an office, not in production, because I like the environment there better. It's completely different, none of that black work, that ink, the regime of the factory, where they have you working from bell to bell. You get there at six, and you stay there till three, till you hear that bell ring again. Where I work now I feel completely different. I'm a free person. I come to work, the girls are there, it's just simpler. There are a lot of interesting people to talk to there, different people, different lives. If you're having problems, the girls try to help you out, they try to calm you down. There are only seven of us in the collective,* in our shift. We sit next to each other, look each other in the

*In Soviet society, the work collective was an important concept, since official ideology placed emphasis on collective experience above the individual. In 1989 several of the teenagers spoke of wanting a good work collective as they envisioned their future employment. For Olya, this has remained an important consideration even as the structure of many workplaces is undergoing considerable change, and public discourse places much greater emphasis on the individual.

eyes. If somebody has had some kind of problem, that's it, everybody knows about it. They ask you what happened, then they tell you to forget about it, it'll be all right. You see, when you're in that kind of situation you do start to feel calmer. You know how nice, how pleasant it is when you are able to make somebody feel better, when you help them or they help you. It's a totally different environment there from the environment in a factory, that's all. It's more like being at home. But that factory, I remember that factory like some horrible dream! I can't imagine how I was able to work there. Even then I didn't like it, I hated going there. Just arriving there made me feel bad. And now I wouldn't go anywhere near that factory! What do I need that for? Printing those little pieces of paper. . . . I'd go there dressed nicely, with a good hairstyle, makeup, and I'd end up putting on those work clothes, that robe, that scarf on my head, my hands covered with ink, always dirty. After working there all day I was a mess, I couldn't go to a restaurant after work the way I can now.

GOING TO WORK VERSUS STAYING IN SCHOOL

I don't want to study anymore. Absolutely not. Why should I continue studying? Let's suppose that I went to an institute or to a technical school, where am I going to go work after that? In production again? Work for the government? Why do I need to do that? Of course not! Study? Definitely not, not for anything. No. Who needs those studies nowadays? Who needs that diploma? Nobody! Right now people are working without having a diploma, making money. The most important thing now is making money, and that diploma is just a piece of paper. Maybe a diploma can help you get a good job someplace, but only in rare cases. For the most part, the average person doesn't find work in the same field that he prepared for. And that's that. Right now at work, the girls I work with, practically all of them have a higher education. One trained as a lawyer, another one has a degree in mechanical engineering. A third has some kind of higher education in computers. All of them have a higher education, except for me! And there we are, working together, doing the same work, getting the same salary! And that's that. I don't know why these girls chose to work there. One of them has a child, so she likes the schedule. People's lives turn out in different ways. And not everybody can get a good job in an enterprise.

I like working there and I have no intentions of leaving, as long as they don't end up closing the place down on us, God forbid, or something like that. I don't plan on leaving. I'll probably stay there until it's time to go on pension. I think I've got myself set unless something better turns up. But to get a better job a person needs a wiser head than the one I've got, and more knowledge than I have, more experience. Maybe with time something better will come up, but I don't know. I'm twenty, so for now I can't resolve that. We'll see in ten years what's going to be!

It seems to me that people who stay in school are now trying to work at the same time, too. It's just the times we live in. It's pretty rare now that somebody can just sit at home and let Mommy and Daddy take care of him, feed him, clothe him, because life has gotten so complex now that the average family just can't make ends meet. The most difficult thing is food, of course, but suppose a young person wants to dress nicely or have some decent shoes, dress fashionably, well then he'll have to go out and start earning a little money somehow. Even if he only works half-days, a few hours a day, something. And if not, well, then he must have the kind of parents who can help out. I suppose a lot depends upon the parents.

It's true I once said that a working person has less freedom than a student, but I don't agree with that now. I think just the opposite! I work, and so I can allow myself to buy or do what I want, more than a person who just studies. I work, so I have money. A student may get a stipend but it's very little.

LOOKING BACK ON THE PTU

If I could go back to the time when I made the decision to leave school and go to the PTU, I would never decide to do that again. Never. I would finish the tenth grade, finish my secondary education, and just go on to work. Because a PTU is neither a school nor a . . . I don't know. It's not anything. The working-class, and that's all. A person gets sent off to the construction site and that's that. I still relate well to the working class personally. What I'm talking about is the way they related to the students, the way they taught us, the atmosphere there, the way it was. There wasn't anything for PTU students to do, they just roamed the streets. There was a lot of crime among the students. To tell you the truth, I think a normal person wouldn't go to a PTU! And if I could go back in time, I wouldn't go either, not for anything. I'd just finish the tenth grade.

So I'm sorry that I chose to go there. But in spite of everything, I was still more mature when I finished there than some of my classmates who went on and finished school. Because you do have a more independent sort of life when you go to a PTU. So yes and no, I regret it and I don't.

If we look at the girls who finished the PTU with me, everybody's life turned out differently. Two girls are on maternity leave and still have some time left, another girl worked at the polygraphic factory but she got married and went on maternity leave. And another girl, the one who had bad vision, she went to work in a household goods store, and then she left that store for another one, a food store. And then she had to leave that store because she came up 12,000 rubles short once at the register, and she was supposed to pay that money somehow. I think she really went through a lot of trouble after she finished that PTU! She managed to pay back the 12,000—can you imagine that? And that wasn't during these times, with these prices, it was still back *then*! And she wanted to get married at that time, and you know how much a wedding costs. She needed that money for her wedding, to set a good table for the guests. And so she got married and now she has a job registering patients at a psychiatric hospital. Working with schizophrenics, epileptics. I asked her why in the world she went to work there, and she said, "Well, where else am I going to get a job?" I tried to get her to come to work with me, where I am, but she didn't want to. Now she's sorry she didn't. And as far as the boys from the PTU go, I don't really know what they're doing. Some of them went back to that factory, the one where we did our practicum. But not the girls. Not even one of them is working there now.

DAILY LIFE

There's only one form of entertainment right now—shopping! Trying to find something to buy. You work one day and you spend the next running around to stores trying to find things. There are always things to be taken care of. And once you start working, well. When you're just studying, you come home after school, do your homework, and you're free. But once you start working, problems appear. Personal problems, problems with relationships—personal relationships and business relationships—and somehow there's no time. I don't seem to have any time. Very little at all. But sometimes I go to cafés and restaurants. Sometimes we go after work. There's a restaurant right across from where I work, where we all know each other. We go there after work, have a bite to eat, and then we visit each other's homes. The same way I used to do, except that this is a different crowd, business people, from work. Business people invite us there to talk things over. We used to go to those places out of curiosity, to get something to eat, to see what those kinds of places were like. Now we go to have a talk. I work now, and I need to relax.

I'm not interested in politics at all. I wasn't before and I'm not now. But I can tell you that everything is pretty bad.

Everything has gotten really expensive. Who knows what's going to happen next? Everybody's gotten so evil, so bitter because of this. Of course we're the first to bear the brunt of all this, the people. And so people's relationships to one another get worse. They're really at each other throats. It's terrible what's going on around here. There's no milk. Nothing for children. No chocolate, fruits, vegetables, milk. Very difficult. Some people will get through it and others will not.

THE BOYFRIEND

I met him at work. He had some business with us, and one day he came up to me said, "Young woman, please give me a pen." I looked at him and I said, "This is not an office-supply station." So he gave me a look and walked away. He thought I was bad-natured and didn't talk to me, just looked at me. He was coming to our office for about half a year. He had some business he was taking care of. And since he was there all the time, he started to notice me. Then one fine day he said to me, "Young woman, could I speak to you for a minute?" So I said okay, and we met. And then he asked me if he could give me a ride home. So I asked him, in what, on public transportation? But he said he had a car out front, so I said yes. I brought my girlfriend along and he drove us to our homes, and then I gave him my phone number. The same day he drove me home he called me up. He said, "Let's go for a drive somewhere." It was in May, two years ago, and the weather was beautiful, like now, sunny. He said, "Let's go for a drive someplace, out to see some nature," and I said, "I'm not going to the countryside, let's just go someplace closer." So he invited me to Zagorsk. In Zagorsk we have some really beautiful churches. I brought along a girlfriend of mine, the same one who got married this year, and we stopped off at the market and bought some fruit, berries, a lot of delicious things, chocolate candies, it was so nice! Imagine, I hadn't

been working there very long, and I had never met a man
like that before, the type who would give me such nice presents as that! We went to Zagorsk. We had a picnic, walked
around, looked at all the churches, but it started to rain, so
we had to leave pretty quickly.

And then he started to show up at my workplace every day,
and we would go to a restaurant to have lunch. And in the
evenings, too, he would come to pick me up and we would go
to another restaurant. We would sit around, eat, talk, and for
me it was really something else, manna from heaven. Here I
was, still a girl, fresh out of the PTU, eighteen years old, and
all of a sudden there was this type of man in front of me,
quite a few years older than I am, and for me, well, it really
opened my eyes to some things in life! And of course, it was
really tempting for me! Naturally I was attracted to him
because I learned a lot from him, saw a lot of things, saw
what my life should be like. He's eighteen years older than I
am.

Then my mother went on vacation. He helped me see her
off. And here I was, alone. Without him things would have
been really difficult, because my mother went off without
leaving me any money. I just had my salary and that wasn't
very much, enough to live on for only a week. I was having a
hard time that year because I had bought a lot of things and I
had a lot of debts. And to pay back my debts, well, where was
I supposed to get the money? I owed about 800 rubles, and
my salary then was about 100 rubles. Where was I supposed
to get that kind of money? I didn't have anyplace to borrow
it. And then he overheard a conversation. My girlfriend was
asking me for the money I owed her, and I said, "Galya, you
know what? I don't have the money to pay you back now." He
heard the whole thing, heard me tell her that as soon as I
had the money I would give it to her. So he said to me, "Olya,
take the money, give it to your girlfriend." So he took me to
her in his car, I gave her the money, and we drove away. I

asked him where he got that kind of money, and he said to me, "Why didn't you tell me right away that you owed her money?" And I told him I didn't feel comfortable talking about it in front of him. I wouldn't have told him if he hadn't overheard it that way.

Anyway, he kept buying things. Fruits, vegetables—it was August by then and there was lots of watermelon. He bought so much we almost had to throw it away, we couldn't eat it all. We had such a romantic summer!

And after that things just went on. We were together for two years. Of course we had arguments, we broke up, got back together, split up again. We used to fight about silly things, like if he didn't show up when he was supposed to, or if I showed up late, got held up someplace with a girlfriend. We fought about those kinds of little things. But it's hard to break up with somebody if you've been together, let's say, a year. And if you've been together all your lives, well, that's really hard!

We lived together for a while in an apartment he rented. My mother was really against my going to live with him. She couldn't understand how I could live with him without getting married. We were going to get married, then we ended up having a month-long fight, and then sometime after New Year's we got together again. Well, not exactly together again, we spoke to each other. It's hard without him. I've gotten used to him. He's gotten used to me, too. He's a very intelligent man, clever, a fine-tuned psychologist who understands people very well. He could always tell what I was thinking about, what I was about to say. He got to know me very well. I used to get surprised and wonder how he understood all of that about me. He's seen a lot in life, that's why.

He's involved in trade. He's been in it for a long time. Even before there were cooperatives, he used to work someplace connected with trade. And now he works in all those commercial things. He's making money!

THE FUTURE

If I get married, if things work out with my boyfriend, if I
know that I will be taken care of, then I want to have a child.
But the way things are, no, I'm not prepared yet, morally or
materially. It's a step of great responsibility to bring a child
into the world. A person really has to think before doing
that. It's a responsibility for your whole life. It's not a toy that
you can just play with and then put aside. It's a child, a part
of your being. You have to make sure that he lives well, has a
happy life.

I want to have a child if I have a husband with a decent
salary and my child will have enough to eat. But as it is now, I
can just barely make ends meet myself. And if I had to live on
my own, and then a child appeared, well, we'd just die. A
child in these circumstances? Never! And I don't know if I'll
find that person. It's hard, given this life of ours.

Here I am, an adult, a grown person. I should have my
own room or my own apartment somewhere, but I still live
with my parents. I'll be here until I get married. And my
father will never leave this apartment. It's really tough, four
people in a two-room apartment. And what will happen when
Alyosha grows up? He's a boy. A girl goes to live with her
husband, but a young man is supposed to bring his bride to
live with him. Where will he bring her? I sleep in one room
with my mother. My brother sleeps in the other room with
my father, but he's gone a lot. We don't talk to each other.
Only a few words, when it's necessary. And we don't eat
together. I never ask him for money because I know he won't
give me any. What a father he is!

WOMEN AND WORK

As long as I like working and I don't have a family, I'll work.
Then we'll see what happens. It seems to me that it's hard to
get by nowadays without working. But I think work is for

men. A woman should stay home if she wants to. A good husband, if he's able to provide for the family, well then, why shouldn't his wife stay at home, and keep busy raising the child? If she really likes working, that's one thing. I think it would be hard for me to sit home and not have anything to do. You go to work, you smile at people, laugh, interact with people. It's interesting. But on the other hand, of course, the work collective where I am now is all female. And you know what that's like! The minute you leave they're all over you. A male collective is better because their tongues don't wag so much. I like my group, but it does have that characteristic. Women need something to talk about. That's just the way it is. They're very gossipy, especially when you're not around!

LIFE, THREE YEARS LATER

Life was simpler and easier three years ago. Everything was cheaper, and you didn't have to knock yourself out trying to find things. So maybe you only got 100 rubles for your salary, but you could still go to a store and find something there to buy. And now I get 1,000 but I can't even afford to buy myself a pair of shoes. I simply can't. What am I supposed to do, save three months' salary to buy a pair of shoes? And then save another three for a pair of boots? And what about everything else? I'm supposed to eat, too!

This is why young people are trying to go into commercial things, to do something on their own, some kind of "business" as they like to say around here. But you need some sort of a foundation for that, first. Money. Connections. Some kind of experience, so you have some idea what you're doing. And how are you supposed to do that? Get it from your friends, your parents? Suppose a little Young Pioneer girl* comes straight from the vocational school and takes it into

---

*The Young Pioneers were the official children's organization in the Soviet Union. The Pioneers had a membership of 25 million children be-

her head to get into business. Well, that's great, but they'll say to her, "What in the world do you think you're doing?" You have to have something to base all that on, I don't even know what. You have to have some kinds of goods or something. If you don't have anything to begin with, it's just a joke to try and get into business.

Even the really big stores are going out of business, so you can imagine what's going on with the little stores these young people start. The big ones are shutting down right and left. The big commercial store that rented space from our agency was open for a year, and then it closed down. Then they rented the space to another store, and it opened up and then it closed down. I certainly don't have any opportunities to get into business. Without any doubt at all, I cannot.

For me what all these changes mean is that I have to worry about money all the time. Things have not gotten any better for me. Only worse. Not many people here would say that things have changed for the better! I suppose there are people who now have the opportunity to make a lot of money, that's true. But I certainly don't. The people who have the chance to make money are making it, but those who don't are just staying in the same spot they've always been in.

Workers are the ones feeling everything first. It's true my mother earns enough, but there is another working class, too. Of course it's not that people are going hungry or that they have no money at all. We're not going hungry here, we have some money. But it's hard to get used to these high prices.

I suppose there is hunger in some places, if on the farms cows are dying, if in the fields the wheat isn't growing, because there is no owner, nobody is responsible. Nobody cares about anything. Nobody does anything. All the people who went to the country to try to do something, to be farm-

---

tween the ages of nine and fourteen. Political education was an important part of Pioneer activities, but for many children the organization served a primarily social and recreational purpose.

ers, to get agriculture going, are returning to the cities. They can't get anything done with those collective farms.* They say, no wheat? Okay. No rye? Nothing? Let's go get a drink! The tractor drivers get drunk and then they start hollering about how they don't have any technology! And that's where the whole problem starts. A cow is meat, milk, cream. And so we don't have meat, milk, cream, because the cows are dying—or the farmers are killing them because they can't make any profit off them.

I think a lot of time will go by before things get better around here. Years. At least five, that's for sure. Things might get worse, but better? Not now. They divided up the country, the Union. When you're together, it's easier, simpler and better. And now, everybody's splitting up, going their own way. Dividing the country up into small pieces. It just makes things with the economy more complicated.

---

*In the Soviet Union, agricultural production was organized into two basic units: the collective farm (*kolkhoz*), in theory owned jointly by its members though largely controlled by the state and the Communist Party; and the state farm (*sovkhoz*), owned by the state. Most agricultural production remains within these two basic forms of ownership. Since agricultural production has been a major difficulty for the Soviet Union and now Russia, land reform and the right to buy, sell, and inherit land is one of the most crucial and controversial issues facing the Russian government. Incentives developed during the period of perestroika were intended to break up the large collective and state farms and encourage small independent farmers. These attempts have been met by many obstacles and great resistance from the directors of collective and state farms.

"SOME KIND OF JUSTICE WILL COME"

LENA

Nineteen years old, second-year student of journalism, Moscow State University

Lena and I get together many times while I am in Moscow. She is still small and thin and all nonstop energy. She wants to know more about everything. She is studying at the university, working full-time, writing articles, learning photography, taking violin lessons, and trying to find a way to go to Denmark to continue the language study she began years ago. She wants to see a bit of the world, she tells me, especially now, since there is no more Soviet Union with its vast borders and diverse cultures. One day she bakes a cake for me, on another she shows me the clothes she has sewn.

Lena wears her hair in the same short style of three years ago, but somehow the boyishness is gone. She dresses neatly and modestly, wears skirts even when we go for a walk in Izmailovsky Park on a Sunday afternoon. The day is hot and sunny and I feel tired and lazy, uninclined toward conversation as we sit on a bench and watch families out in paddleboats on a small lake. But Lena wants to talk about religion and philosophy and how a person can find meaning in life without a god. There is an urgency to her rapid-fire questions: she wants to understand the world. She will leave no subject uncovered before my departure from Moscow, as if she is storing up our conversations for some later contemplation. Lena is going to go very far, I think. If she were a student in a class of mine, I would have a hard time keeping up with her.

LENA

After I finished school I tried to get into the Journalism Department at Moscow State University, just as I had been planning. I took all the exams, but it's very competitive, there are lots of students trying to get in, and I didn't. You had to get 5s[*] in all the exams. But even if you answer all the questions, well they're still not going to give everyone a 5. They have only a certain number of students they can accept in each department. In the daytime section of the Journalism Department they take only 170 students, but there are 500 trying to get in. They have to select the students, they sift through them. So I ended up having to go out to work instead of studying.

I got a job at a small newspaper that belongs to the Moscow Engineering and Construction Institute. They have their own small newspaper. I worked as a reporter, a photographer, and then I did all kinds of technical work, putting the newspaper together, paste-up, illustration. It was great practice for me! I worked there one whole year. And during that year I slowly and steadily got myself prepared for the next summer's exams. I studied. And the next year I was accepted at the Journalism Department, but only in the correspondence section. We have three sections. One, the regular daytime, when all you do is study. Then there's the evening section, where you have a job during the day and at night you study at the school. And then there's the correspondence section, where you study, but independently. You get the program, study it, and you only show up at the institute to take your exams.

I've finished the first year there. Since it's considered more difficult to study on your own, the program is a year longer. I'll be there six years. I can work while I'm studying. Actually, our economic situation at the moment doesn't allow me *not* to work! I work at the Gorky Film Studio, where I retouch photos in the department of animated films for children. As I

*The highest grade in a system of 1–5.

told you three years ago, I want to be a photographer, and where I'm studying now, there is no photojournalism. I can't train for the profession I want. So I went to work in the photography department of the film studio. And maybe there I'll be able to learn, little by little, how to be a photographer.

This summer I wanted to enter a technical school for photography. But I had already given my original documents—the certificate that said I had finished secondary education, and my medical certificate—to the university in order to enroll, and the technical school refused to take a photocopy. The originals have to stay on file at the university until I graduate. So because of bureaucracy you can only study in one institute at a time, even though officially you're allowed to study in more than one. But I could have done it! I would have enrolled in the evening section at that technical school. In two years I would be a photographer, and in six years I would get my diploma in journalism. I really liked that idea. But our system doesn't allow it!

But the real problem is related to the problem of our whole system of education. I'm now almost twenty years old. Where you come from, a person is probably already pretty independent by that age, already wants something from life, and probably has already accomplished something. But here, what do we have to show for our ten years of schooling? What knowledge do we have?

Our schools don't prepare us. If you want to get into a technically oriented VUZ, you have to take extra courses in mathematics, outside of school, just so you can be admitted! Or if you want to get into the History Department, you have to take extra courses in order to get in. I'm nineteen years old, I've gone through ten years of schooling, one at the university, and there isn't a single subject about which I can say I have any in-depth knowledge!

I'm supposed to be learning something at Moscow State University. But really I am not satisfied with the way we are taught. We have a lot of required subjects and so many of them are just unnecessary! For example, we have a subject called "Technical Tools of the Journalist." We spent a whole year studying the "Technical Tools of the Journalist." And what are those tools? A ballpoint pen and a piece of paper! A dictaphone and a camera! And we take a whole year to study that, and take an exam in it! Look, I worked at a newspaper for a year right after I graduated from secondary school. And I learned all of that right away, at work. I don't need to get any theoretical knowledge of that! It is just totally obvious and self-evident that a journalist writes with a pen, carries around a pen, and knows how to read and write, uses a tape recorder, a camera, and a video camera! And we have a lot of subjects like that, in every institute.

We don't have those other courses any more, though—Marxist-Leninist philosophy, history of the Communist Party of the Soviet Union, all that. But for seventy years that Marxist-Leninist philosophy was the most important subject, no matter what institute you were in! And the Journalism Department was the most Marxist-Leninist department, completely based on that Marxism-Leninism-Partyism, and now that they've taken that away, everything that was based upon that subject has just disappeared into thin air. And you can really feel it.

The first semester we studied ancient Russian literature, at breakneck speed. The first literary works, before the twelfth century, all those old manuscripts. A tremendous amount of really fascinating material. You'd need a minimum of a year or two just to get a grip on it. But we took only half a year for it and we'll never return to that subject again. I found it so interesting, I liked studying it, and suppose I'd like to continue studying that, take a seminar in it, learn more. But we'll never go back to it.

And that's what really bothers me. A whole year has gone by. How much I could have learned, discovered, during that year! But instead I had to spend a lot of time studying all those useless courses. "Technical Tools of the Journalist!"

Nobody needs to study that. Our textbooks are all so old, and technology has already gone on ahead. The equipment in television and in radio is already so different, completely different.

I've been studying violin for about a month now, because I never finished music school. I just kept thinking about what I'd missed out on, all those ten years in school. I had wanted to learn a language. But after all that time we spent on it in school, what do we know? The English alphabet and the most simple, basic things. "I live in Moscow. My name is Lena." So I learned Danish on my own. I took a course in it. And after two years I know Danish better than I know English, because I took the course on my own initiative.

My parents got a good education. When she was my age my mother studied German for four years at the Institute of Foreign Languages, and now she's fifty years old and she still knows German really well. And I wasted six years learning English in school and I can't say anything more than "My name is Lena"!

This is going to be a problem, when our whole generation grows up uneducated. I can see this in journalism. Of the people who are studying in the same year as I am, some are working in television, some in radio, because they have already been set up, had help from their parents or somebody. And they have such a youthful pride that they work in television, that they don't really need to get an education, that they already know everything, know how to do everything. And this is already evident in television programs. There are young people on the shows who don't know how to carry themselves. They need to learn this, too! If a person is educated, you can see that in the way that he conducts an interview. And if a correspondent isn't educated, doesn't know what he's doing, then even an interview with an interesting person doesn't work out, because the journalist doesn't know what to ask or how to communicate. I think it's just gotten very fashionable now to hand over the screen to

young people! Radio to the young people, newspapers to
the young people!

Look, that Stalinist system—no, not just Stalinist, but the
whole Soviet system in general—for all the terrible things it
had, the way it kept people in line through force, still had its
positive sides. Education, for example. Now people have
started paying for their diplomas. That didn't happen before.
You just show up, pay money, and buy a diploma! At the
Medical Institute! Even though you never really studied
there. And it costs a lot of money. But we have that category
of people now, people who can buy themselves a diploma
from an institution of higher education.

Before, if a person was smart, was talented, wanted to do
something in his field, was a young, energetic person, well, if
he wanted to have any kind of success, he had to join the
Komsomol* and the Party, pledge himself to that. It was necessary for his career, just to join. Things have changed for us.
We don't have to belong to any party, but now if you have
money, doors are open for you. And if you have money plus
talent, you'll achieve what you want. And in general, even in
the absence of talent, if you have money, that's the most
important thing, and you'll be successful. And of course
that's a shame. It's not even that it's just or unjust, it just
makes me feel sorry for my country!

But I think it's only now, in these first waves, this muddle,
that a talentless person can get something because he en-
gages in speculation, the mafia, those kinds of things. But
really, it seems to me that this can't go on very much longer.
Because even if a person is poor, he may be much more talented, much more humane and interesting than someone

---

*The Komsomol was the official Soviet organization for young adults
between the ages of fourteen and twenty-eight. It had a fundamental role
in the ideological development of Soviet citizens and had considerable
resources. By the 1970s, however, the Komsomol was seen by most young
adults as a stepping stone to university admission or career advancement.

with money. And maybe with time, as things stabilize, with a little more justice maybe someone like that will also be able to achieve something. Some kind of justice will come. Not immediately, not today, but in five, ten years. I really do believe quite strongly that Russia is going to play a role for the good of the whole world. I really think that. I, for example, will never leave Russia. Never. I could go someplace to visit, to study for awhile, see the world. But I will always, no matter what, return. I couldn't live in another country. The Russian character, it seems to me, is really different from all others.

Despite everything, people here are open. Even in difficult situations, like the Revolution, the Second World War, people get together, collect themselves. Even if they hide these qualities in themselves for a time, these qualities in people don't die, they're just hidden. I think I already said, in the book, that this is a country of paradox! And it is going to stay that way. That is, there will always be poverty and wealth, justice and injustice, there will always be talentless people, greedy people, but there will also always be talented people, generous people. It will always be like that here.

CAREER

I had the idea of studying journalism three years ago. But since that time my views of life and my future profession have changed and I've become a little disillusioned with journalism. I do like journalism as a profession, especially photojournalism, but maybe it's the way things are here now. Let me try to explain. I like doing interviews and then writing an article about them, or writing historical articles, based on some kind of research. But I worked for one year at a small newspaper and I didn't really like that journalism. This profession seems a little superficial, because you can't know about everything in a deep way. When you're writing an article, you have to read something about that material, know something about it, learn something. But if I am going to write about a particular topic, I have to really know the issues and for that you need a lot of time. But in our modern newspapers, you don't get that much time; they give you a fixed deadline. But I'm not the kind of person who can write immediately, just by taking a quick look at what's happened, and come up with conclusions. First I have to delve into things, take a look at one side of the issue, then the other, witness things, hear one person's opinion and then another's, read something about it, and only then can I make my own conclusions. But newspapers, radio, and television don't give you that kind of time. I don't think I could be a television journalist or a radio journalist. Not even if I would learn how to look wonderful in front of a camera. I just can't speak about something when I am not absolutely certain that things really are the way I'm saying.

When I was working at the newspaper, they would give me a certain topic, and the whole time they would be after me, saying, "Come on, come on, hurry up!" For example, once there was an article written in the newspaper *Moscow Komsomol* about the institute where I worked, the Engineering and Construction Institute, where the newspaper was from. The article said that they had found some radioactive contamination in a classroom in one of the institute buildings. That article said that everybody there was already contaminated, the students, the teachers, everybody had already positively started to glow from all that radioactivity! But I started to study the problem, went to that building, and as it turns out everything was much simpler and not nearly as horrible as they were saying. In one very small portion of one wall there was a small radioactive element, but completely enclosed within cement and not dangerous because nobody was exposed to it. A tiny amount that in general didn't even exceed the safety norms for radioactivity. And the teachers who had been working there for twenty, thirty, forty years were all healthy and had healthy children and there wasn't

anything terrible in those classrooms where they had been
teaching for so many years. But some students had taken an
instrument to the wall and discovered that in one part of it,
you would get a reading that was a little higher than the naturally occurring radioactivity. It wasn't very dangerous. And it
was really insulting to me that people got so worked up about
it, that such a panic began. The students stopped going to
classes because they were afraid, parents wouldn't let their little kids walk on the path that goes right by the building, to
their kindergarten. They were scared that their children
would be contaminated! But if that journalist would really
have gone there and gotten to the bottom of the matter, gone
to specialists who know about radioactivity and construction
materials, well, things wouldn't haven't developed that way.
People wouldn't have gotten so nervous because of that article, and that panic that began immediately wouldn't have
everybody thinking, "Oh, we've been contaminated!" And
they would have gone on studying.

And the whole time I was studying the problem, the newspaper was after me, "Come on, faster, faster!" But it was difficult for me to work faster. It was a very specific kind of question and I'm not a specialist in that matter, so I had to go to
the department and talk to people, and talk to people from a
special committee that had been formed to investigate, and I
had to look at all their reports. So that's why I don't think I
have the temperament to be a journalist.

And then journalists have to be pretty nervy and rude, in
the good sense of the word, have to turn up in places where
they're not supposed to be, ask things they're not supposed
to, and be tactless at times, a little unethical in their relationships to people. And I'm not really like that. I feel uncomfortable taking people away from their work, for example, when
they're busy and I am supposed to do an interview. It's hard
for me to understand why a person should interrupt his
work, take time off to answer my questions. What right do I

have to do that? I think you have to have that characteristic in your personality, and I don't think I really do. That's why I think photojournalism is closer to me, in the first place because I really enjoy photography and also because if you are doing a story silently, taking pictures, that's simpler. And the reader, who will see the photos, will draw his own conclusions. He'll see for himself. Of course I can make a commentary, but basically I won't be forced to bother people, ask them all sorts of tactless questions.

I do think that journalism is still playing an important role in this society, the way it was three years ago, but now all these magazines, newspapers are being sold on every corner, and it's difficult to figure them all out and know whether or not they really show good quality, both technically and in terms of their content. There are some pretty coarse papers out there now. Sensational, vulgar, there's a lot of them. I think *Moscow Komsomol* is one of those, like the article it had about the institute where I was working. It was clear just from reading it that the journalist who had written the article really wasn't informed, he was just paying attention to a lot of rumors. Even the name of the president of our institute was wrong, and the names of a lot of the teachers there too, and then the names of the departments weren't really the right ones either. I didn't like that at all.

So even though at the moment I'm studying in the Journalism Department, I'm trying not to get too deeply involved in the specialized courses and really am trying to get a good general, well-rounded education, outside of the university. Literature, history, music—I study on my own—and I'd also like to learn how to draw. And then I have the idea that I really want to study languages. Like Danish, even though now I don't get any practice at all. But I have this idea—who knows if it will work out—that I should write to some Danish institution of higher education and see if I could get some kind of practice there, maybe even study there.

THE CURRENT SITUATION

We're living in such a time of contrasts now. There is enormous general impoverishment and misery, and at the same
time a lot of millionaires have appeared. A very sharp division. And this division doesn't depend upon one's education, professional qualities, or age. People our age might be
working in a cooperative, selling some kind of rags at a high
price, or get involved with speculation, and they can earn several thousand, just like that. It doesn't matter what age they
are, what level they're at professionally.

There are so many people here who have become so pessimistic; they're in a total state of depression. They're leaving
their jobs, they're dissatisfied, they're unhappy with the
prices, with the lines. And yet I also see a big wave of enthusiasm, a desire to change things, and things have turned
around really quickly. It used to seem that, well, whether or
not they were satisfied, people got more or less the same pay,
lived more or less in the same way, had the same opportunities for dachas, cars, furniture; but now the idea of getting a
dacha, a car, or an apartment has become unrealistic for most
people. Still, there are opportunities for people to direct their
energies to something else. Because financially, well, we can't
afford to buy an apartment, we can't even dream about it anymore! With the salaries we earn today it won't be possible in
ten, or even twenty or thirty years. That's why we don't even
think about it anymore. So now the only thing to think about
is spiritual pursuits, not material things.

Our country could be a lot richer than it is, but we don't
know how to use our wealth. I think we told you three years
ago that when we would go work in the summer harvesting
vegetables, how many fields of rotting produce we saw. Fields
and fields of tomatoes, all burned from the sun because
nobody had harvested them, or beets, carrots, cucumbers, all
of them. Fields of unharvested vegetables, because there is
no manpower to harvest them! But then we pay so much

money to buy from you those same tomatoes we leave rotting in the field! So we have a lot of wealth. But we waste it. It's related to our psychology. We're different from you. Judging from the programs I've seen about your society, a young man my age over there, he already knows that if he doesn't study well, he won't get an education, and he won't get a job, he'll have very little money and he won't live well. Here it's just the opposite. A young man thinks, "How can I manage things so that I won't have to study, won't have to work?" He tries to be clever enough to not have to do anything, or to do less but somehow still have more. I think it's connected to our systems. It's psychological. Here, if somebody's building a house and he doesn't have any bricks, he'll run over to a construction site and just take them. They're just lying around anyhow. And who cares if there aren't enough for the construction site, as long as you have what you need? Our attitudes toward things are simply different.

I have become very disillusioned with our government. April first, last year [1991], Pavlov's* reforms started—the increase in prices, I think only nine-tenths of a percent. And people got really upset and they got rid of him. But in comparison to those reforms, what our government is doing now—people don't even notice anymore what prices are! Today bread costs 1 ruble, tomorrow 5 rubles, maybe it will go up to 100. I think people have simply gotten tired. People had such high spirits during the coup, and afterward, the mood when they won was so happy. It wasn't even clear *what* they had won, but everybody felt that they were defending democracy, and thought that the coup really changed things, that now we were really going to have democracy, freedom, that all these things were really just beginning. And that's why people were ready to sacrifice so much. The mood in

---

*Valentin Pavlov, the conservative USSR minister of finance who became prime minister in January 1991, was a key participant in the August 1991 coup attempt.

Moscow then was really impressive. People were in the streets, building barricades spontaneously, and without anybody telling them what to do. Nobody was ordering anybody to do anything. At night people stayed there on guard duty, even though the weather was terrible. They huddled under umbrellas, they lit fires, they felt that they were defending democracy.

And the people did what needed to be done. They defended the government, they did everything they could to defend the government, so that the government could go ahead and do its work peacefully. But the government didn't really appreciate or fully understand what the people had sacrificed. The people really gave everything, sincerely—not everybody of course, but many people.

Some even gave their lives! Things like that had happened elsewhere, perhaps, in the Baltics, or in Georgia, or in Karabakh, but somehow it had not caught up to us. And then people experienced it, even a curfew during that first day. You couldn't go out into the streets after eleven at night, because there were armed battalions cruising around, and they were authorized to use their arms at any time. But despite that, people were ready to encircle the White House* with their own bodies, and storm it. We hadn't seen that before. They had tanks and helicopters around the White House! People didn't know what would happen. There were so many tanks. But they were ready to go to their death. Women were there. And then there was a priest there, dressed in his church robes, and he blessed all the people who were there. There hadn't been anything like that around here before! The soul was awakened in people who had been asleep for years! Such a surge of patriotism! And not just for Yeltsin. People felt they were doing it for themselves.

But it was unfinished, there was no conclusion. The government never thanked the people. And I think that was

_____

*The seat of the Russian government.

Yeltsin's mistake. He accepted all that sacrifice as if it were owed to him. People were ready to go to their death for him, and he, well, I didn't like his response. He didn't know how to manage and direct that surge of the people's enthusiasm somehow, to do something else, to get people back to work. He should have thought, "Well, we've won, now we have to get everybody together, to rebuild everything that's been destroyed." All Moscow was covered with those barricades. The government should have done all this, but it didn't. Just the opposite. And as a result of this tremendous amount of energy that never found any channel, whole masses of people went around Moscow defacing things, tearing down monuments, Dzerzhinsky, Lenin. That was all on account of this tremendous surge of energy. I myself was expecting something of Yeltsin. Something should have happened.

I think Yeltsin's inability to really do something stems from his lack of true culture. Look, if you consider all our leaders—well, I mean our tsars, they were well educated. But all of our leaders from the Party didn't have that. Yeltsin comes from the Communist Party, and Gorbachev did too. They don't have a high enough level of culture or education. We were at the funeral of those three young men who were killed during the coup. Well, I was just shocked at the way Yeltsin didn't pay attention to them, to people who gave up their lives for him. They went out into the street so that he could stay in power. One was run over by a tank, another was shot, and our leader, who remained among the living, should have come out and honored them, given some sign. Which, by the way, Gorbachev did. Everybody was out, the whole square was full, all of Moscow came out to bury those young men, near Manezh Square. Gorbachev was there, and Sakharov's* widow, Bonner, and the American ambassador, Strauss, and Afghan veterans, and it was hot, summer,

---

*Andrei Sakharov, the noted physicist and political dissident, famous both for his role in developing the Soviet Union's atom bomb and for his

August. And after everybody, from President Gorbachev to
the Afghan veterans, had spoken their piece, had honored
the dead, they carried those caskets through Moscow to the
White House so that Yeltsin would come and stand out on
the balcony and say something. And we were there, and as
we got closer to the White House, it was terrible. We could
see that everybody around us was forgetting about those
caskets and those dead boys. They started running faster,
toward the White House, just so that they could get a look
at Yeltsin. It was so shocking that we simply left. It was really
an unpleasant thing, when somebody has given up their life
for someone else, and that person goes ahead and makes
some kind of show out of it. I think Yeltsin's gesture, in that
instance, was a negative indication of his character.

Of course one can't diminish the role Yeltsin played during the coup. He organized everything. As a man, in an
extreme situation, in an emergency, he knows what to do. He
didn't let people panic during the coup. He kept things in
control. But afterward, when the emergency was over, he
didn't really know what to do. He doesn't know what to do
under ordinary circumstances. After the coup he did things
like banning the Communist Party and closing down certain
newspapers, useless things. During a coup you might have to
do things like that, it's a kind of war. But under ordinary circumstances, other things are needed.

I don't like the way Yeltsin handled himself around Gorbachev, how he treated him when he arrived from the
Crimea.* You could see what a difficult moral situation Gorbachev was in. Maybe he was just putting on a show for the

---

subsequent criticism of Soviet military and foreign policies, including its
participation in the war in Afghanistan. Sentenced to exile in the city of
Gorky by Leonid Brezhnev, Sakharov was later freed by Mikhail Gorbachev
and returned to Moscow where he played an important role in political
and public life until his death in December 1989.

*Gorbachev had been vacationing in the Crimea and was held captive
there during the coup. He returned to Moscow after the coup was defeated.

public, but it seemed to me that he was sincere. He's the kind of person who is very susceptible to the influence of others. When he was the head of government he was always . . . Well, Sakharov would speak, then Lukyanov,* others, and somehow he would be in agreement with one, and then somehow with the other. And he really wanted something to come out of all of this. I don't think that he wanted to harm his people in any way with his perestroika. But as it turned out, things really were destroyed. And now that things aren't so sweet around here, life is so hard. Well, in a way that's a result of Gorbachev. He created the circumstances for this collapse. But the tragedy for many people here is that they lived in a certain way all their lives, Gorbachev, too, and he wanted to do something good for people. But now people are cursing at him. When he came from the Crimea he was in a state of shock—after all, he had been betrayed by his best, closest friends. He and Lukyanov had studied together, were in college together, began their careers together. How could he not trust in him? And it seems to me that when a person is in a state of shock like that, he needs to be given time, to collect himself. But immediately Yeltsin started to go after him. Ban the Communist Party! Leave the Communist Party! And Gorbachev needed time. Maybe in a few days he would have come to that conclusion himself. But that gesture of Yeltsin's, that vulgar gesture, right there on the tribune, Yeltsin signed and read aloud that decree about the Communist Party, and the whole auditorium stood up and applauded, and Gorbachev stood there, betrayed, defeated. You could see Yeltsin had no respect for Gorbachev at all. Even if he didn't agree with him, he should have had some respect! The whole thing was done so crudely.

And then later, that whole thing about the nuclear briefcase, with the buttons, really could have been done in a dif-

---

*Anatoly Lukyanov, chairman of the USSR Supreme Soviet, was involved in the coup of August 1991.

ferent way. Officially. With some ceremony. They could have
had an official meeting. They could have taken down the Red
flag and slowly raised the Russian flag, Gorbachev could
have turned everything over to Yeltsin, something like that.
Even if it were just being done for the public, it should have
been done in a humane way! Instead it was done in a way
that showed a lack of culture. There are some norms of
human behavior. People have to relate reasonably to the mistakes of the past.

THE FUTURE

I have already prepared myself to expect that my life is going
to be difficult. In the material sense, definitely, that's the way
it's always been here. It's already a tradition, a national
characteristic: we are always lacking something! In this
century and the last century, something's always missing. If
life is too easy, it's not interesting. For example, I probably
couldn't live in America! Of course you've got problems,
but . . .

Personally, I don't think I'll work as a journalist. I like the
profession, but not in this country. So I can't say that I've
chosen a profession. I chose a department to study in. I'll
choose my profession later. I'm trying to learn photography
and I'm making some small steps. We'll see if that works out.
In the meantime I'm continuing with music, learning the violin, and later I'll study more. I'd like to keep studying some
philosophy, religion, history.

MARRIAGE AND FAMILY

I imagine that forming a family is not going to be easy. Three
years ago I had pretty big expectations, of myself and of my
future husband, and in the last three years these expectations
have grown even more. I still have not met a person who is
spiritually suited—and I'm not even talking about material cir-

cumstances, because in our country nothing is stable in that sense anyhow. Maybe today I'll bring home an enormous amount—well, let's just say that in this country there are a thousand ways to earn money—but at the same time there are a thousand ways to lose everything as well! Life is so complicated that I am not even going to talk about the material aspect of life. But as far as those spiritual things that bind a family, well, in this regard I have very high demands. And I don't know if I'll be able to fulfill them because I haven't met anybody yet who comes close to this, for whom the spiritual side of life has great significance. Young people are all thinking about money, about how to make money.

And then I have my own view about raising children, about children in a family, about children as independent personalities, and in general I haven't met any young men who share those views. And in general, I doubt that young men here are thinking about children at all.

I've met some young men. I'm not saying that they are all bad. There are many cheerful, interesting ones, but just as friends. I'm glad they're my friends. But as far as a husband is concerned, a life companion, father of my future children, well, I haven't met that kind of young man yet.

But I'm in the process of searching for one! Because if you don't look, you won't find! And of course a search by definition brings with it some mistakes. I think I'll recognize the person who meets my expectations if I've already made a few mistakes along the way. I'll be able to judge better, appreciate better. Oh yes, I'm definitely in the active process of searching for one!

But maybe because I have two older brothers, since childhood I've been accustomed to being surrounded by men who are older than I am. And I relate to my brothers as if we were all equals. I have to say that I think my brothers are on a higher level than the average young man. My oldest brother is really talented. He could have been a good actor, but life just turned out so that he didn't become one. Still, he's really

exceptionally talented. He has his own family, and even my
nephew has an actor's talents! My second brother, Andrei, is
also a very talented man, but again his life turned out so that
he can't realize some of his own capabilities, because he just
got married and they're expecting a baby. I think he's very
talented in philosophy, history, literature—he has very interesting ideas and unusual approaches to these things. But
maybe with time—he's only twenty-four, almost twenty-five—
maybe he'll find his chance.

My brothers really influenced my ideas of what a young
man should be like. The communication with my brothers
has had a big, decisive role in shaping what I want. They are
so interesting to talk to, and we've traveled all over the place
together. Andrei, especially, has talked to me a lot about
things. He's not traditional, he's unusual. And somehow this
has affected the way I look at young men. I judge the young
men I meet by the same standards I apply to my older brothers. And I have high expectations of myself too! Maybe young
men don't really like that.

I don't think I'll find the person I will want to spend the
rest of my life with just like that, that one meeting will be
enough to convince me that that person is my life companion. Sometimes a first impression can be mistaken. Sometimes you need more contact to start seeing sides of a person
you hadn't seen at first. I don't think it's immoral to have
relationships while you're looking for a life companion. I'm
not in a hurry! I'm looking, quietly and thoughtfully. I don't
like it when every time a girl meets a young man she's
already looking at it from that point of view—is he the one or
isn't he? But I suppose it's true that every young man you
meet, whether it's at work or school or even at the bus stop,
becomes part of that experience. And even a bad experience
is experience. Let's suppose I meet some young man, and
things don't work out and we break up. Even that experience
will have some meaning in my life. I might look at myself a
little differently. Or maybe I'll realize that I need to change

some of my expectations, or maybe just the opposite, I'll confirm some of them. But in any case I don't consider it a waste of time. Everything has its meaning. And its time.

When I look at the young men who graduated school with me, or who study with me at the university, I realize that the socialist education we received, or whatever you'd call it, affected the relationships between men and women. Women are supposed to dress, wash and iron clothes, feed him, and in addition work and raise the children. All that for a man as if it were an obligation, even though she works too.

It's true that people get married young here, even though it's hard to raise a family now. But they're getting married anyway, even though they know they're going to have difficulties with money, with an apartment, with everything! If they knew that in ten years, let's say, when they were twenty-eight, that they'd be able to get an apartment and provide for a family, then maybe young people here wouldn't be in such a hurry to get married, it wouldn't be as much of a goal. But when you already know beforehand that in ten years, twenty years, thirty years . . . and your parents know that their children, to the end of their lives, will depend on them—then there's no sense in waiting until you're twenty-five or so. Why wait? You're still going to be dependent. And in any case, it's easier for parents and grown children to live together. We have so many complications to life here, it's hard to get around them living by yourself! That's a specifically Soviet thing! One of our characteristics. It isn't that way in the West.

In Russia it was always accepted that people lived together in big families. It wasn't normal for children to leave their parents' homes. Rather, a young husband in some Russian village would bring his young bride to live with his family. And his children would do the same, bring their spouses to live with them. People lived in big families, with all the children, grandchildren, the old folks. And wives were always dependent on their husbands. It's remained that way. In the majority of cases here, a wife is dependent on her husband, for some things. Psychologically. Materially. For example, when a child is born, the woman gets three years of maternity leave. They pay here for that, but of course it's a very small amount of money. The money is so little that without a man it would be very difficult for her to stay at home and take care of the child, to raise it, get it on its feet.

DAILY LIFE

Dad was laid off from his job as a television film director. There was a campaign, and they laid off everybody who had worked for television. Television used to belong to the state, but then that was abolished and the people were automatically laid off. Now we have Russian television instead—the Ostankino television company. Dad works at the same place, but it's called the Ostankino television company. He works there in the Political Studio. He just came back from a business trip to Chelyabinsk 2, a closed city full of nuclear scientists, to make a film about the "brain drain" that's now taking place in the former Soviet Union. Many of the good specialists are leaving and going abroad. He's making a series of television programs about this.

In general he has the same work problems everybody has now. They pay him irregularly. But at least he got a raise. I think he's earning 2,000 or 3,000, which is not really very much. And Mom is earning about 1,200. So in my family we don't really have much money, especially considering that we're paid irregularly. Dad has been back at the television station since February and they just paid him his first salary a week ago—after more than three months!

I haven't been paid this month either. On May 24 we were supposed to get half our pay for June as an advance, but they didn't pay us. Then they promised to pay us around June 12. So they haven't paid us our May salary or our advance, because there's no money in the banks now, and our studio doesn't have any money either. I don't know, maybe by the end of June we'll get our money for May! And that's not even a sure thing. I get 920 rubles a month. I got a part of my salary this month and it's already been spent, and I have to get to the end of the month somehow. Maybe I'll borrow some money from my brother Andrei.

I buy my own books and I pay for my music lessons, and really I am paying for my own food now, too. We all buy food together really. I buy some things, they do the same. We don't pool our money to keep the household running. Dad buys something, Mom buys something at work, I buy something. But my parents are working a lot now to earn more money. They work on vacation days and holidays because they get paid double to work then. They worked on all the holidays in May—Workers' Day, Victory Day. And I worked, too. We're all working a lot.

I couldn't just study now, without working. In the first place, I've gotten used to working. Last year, when I wasn't accepted into the university and I started to work, I got used to being able to pay my own way. It's not that I can buy myself anything expensive, but can I pay for my own food and the basic things I need to live. And in the situation we're in now it would be hard for me to take money from my parents. Maybe if I had gotten into the university right away, and had been accepted into the daytime classes, it would be easier for me just to study and not work. But now I've gotten used to working. It's a completely different regime and I like it. I feel more self-confident when I don't have to ask my parents for money for something very basic or even for a book, for lunch, whatever. This way I know I can handle my own money, and I can even buy my parents some things.

I earn a miserable salary though. I can't buy myself shoes, I can't even buy myself stockings, they're so expensive now—150 rubles, and even at that price you can't find them. I'm in a situation where I can't buy myself much. But I'm pretty relaxed about that. Somehow I have things. I sew things, or alter some of my mother's things. I don't feel like I have a big problem with that.

When the first price increase took place in January, people spent a whole month just walking around in shock. Right away prices went up five or six times. Bread cost 20 kopecks and then all of a sudden it cost 2 or 3 rubles. People had certain habits, so then they were shocked. But then prices continued going up and up and people got used to it. Sugar cost 1 ruble a kilo, and then suddenly it went up to 7 rubles, then 24, and now there it is for 84! The same for cheese, and butter. Butter used to cost 3.5 a kilo, then all of a sudden to 10, and then it went up to 70 rubles. Now it's about 200. Maybe that seems like pennies if you translate it into dollars, but with our salaries, it's a lot. Right now my whole monthly salary would buy me 4 kilos of butter! Meat is difficult to find in stores right now, but you can buy it at the farmer's market for 300 rubles a kilo. So I can allow myself to buy 3 kilos of meat with my entire monthly salary! And that's it.

I live at home so I don't need to spend a lot on myself, but I am taking private violin lessons and that costs 80 rubles a week. Almost 400 rubles of my 900 goes to pay for the violin lessons, so I have 500 left over. But I only got paid 700 in May. And of course I have to spend money to get to work, and then to eat something in the middle of the day. Also, I buy a lot of books, and books are very expensive now. It's going to be Mom's birthday soon, and mine, too, and that costs a lot of money. Just to have people over for tea and cake costs a lot. And then presents, flowers—I like to do something nice for Mom, buy her something. I don't mind spending money for that, but I simply don't have it!

For a lot of people these problems are the most important. Mom and I went on a trip with a group of people from her job. We went to Vilnius and Warsaw. One day in Vilnius, one day in Warsaw, back to Vilnius for a day, and then back to Moscow. And we didn't have any money! We were supposed to change money for each day, 25,000 zlotys—that's about one bottle of vodka. There were girls my age who went on this trip with huge bags full of things to sell, all kinds of things, and the one day we had in Warsaw—the *one and only day* we had in that beautiful city!—well, they spent the whole day by the train station, near that huge market, trying to sell as much as they could. And then, with whatever amount of those pathetic zlotys they made they tried to buy things in Poland. I don't even remember what it was they were trying to buy. Some kind of tea services, I think. They were so tired and irritable after that, and they didn't even see the city!

But Mom and I changed our 25,000 zlotys in an hour and bought our bottle of vodka or whatever, and then went out all day to see the city. We had a little money left over so we each bought a banana! But we had a great time. The historic center of Warsaw is really beautiful and we spent the whole day just walking around and really got a lot of pleasure from that! In contrast to our Russian compatriots and their trading . . . Well, everybody has their own goals in life, their own relationship to life.

—

"I DON'T LIKE LIVING MY LIFE ACCORDING TO THE PLAN"

ILYA

*Nineteen years old, fourth-year student of Russian
language and literature, Moscow State University*

*Ilya is busy: his wife, Sasha, who is having a difficult pregnancy, is
in the hospital for observation, and Ilya is still in the middle of
final exams at the university. But he finds a free evening and
invites me to the apartment that had been his mother's, where he
and Sasha now live alone. When he opens the door, I am surprised
to see how much he has changed. There is no trace of a teenager
anymore: he has grown much taller and I have to look up to meet
his smile. He has long hair and dresses in the hippie style so common among the young men at Moscow State. His face is still soft
and delicate but his smile is warmer and the polite distance is gone.
We are friends. Equals.*

*Ilya seems happy about the new kinship between us. He has been
on a trip to Chicago, where I now live, and we talk about the city,
about Evanston, where he stayed, and about the American lifestyle.
But more important, we are both going to become parents in the
fall. Perhaps because of the difficulties Sasha is experiencing, Ilya is
worried about me, asks me repeatedly about my health, and offers to
feed me at least three times during the course of our conversation.
He asks me if I still care about politics or if I have "more important" things to worry about now. I remind him that three years ago
he thought there was nothing more important than politics, and he*

ILYA

laughs. He is excited about the baby, tells me they have found out it will be a boy.

At ten o'clock I decide I must leave; I have been warned that it is no longer safe to walk the Moscow streets at night, especially for people who "look like foreigners." But Ilya insists that I eat first, and he fries the cabbage, potato, and meat piroshki he has bought specially for our reunion. The piroshki are warm and buttery and we drink hot tea. There are even chocolate candies that I know must have been difficult to find and very expensive. Over the food we talk about patriarchy, feminism, and gender roles, and Ilya tells me that my ideas are very mistaken, that men and women are profoundly different and will always remain that way, that feminism tries to make them the same. I tell him how happy I am to see how clean and orderly he manages to keep his house, and what a nurturer he has become.

We are sad to say good-bye. He wishes me good luck, and we promise to let each other know when the babies arrive.

When you left Moscow three years ago I was worried about getting into the university. It seemed so difficult to me then, so complicated, but now it seems so long ago, and not nearly as complicated as it seemed then. I got into the university and right away I got involved with student life, which is really wonderful.

Then I went to Chicago. When I was still in school I had participated in a television game, a literary competition, and our school's team won. As a prize we got a week's trip to Denmark. We were really lucky. We all liked Denmark a lot. And then a game was organized in Moscow with an American team put together by a professor from Northwestern University in Evanston. The Americans were here for ten days and we showed them Moscow. Then, a month later, we went to Chicago, also for ten days, and the game went on, but of course the game wasn't the most important thing! I was already a first-year student at the university at the time of the trip to Chicago, so I wasn't really supposed to be part of the school team anymore. Anyway, I was so impressed with

Chicago! For a whole month after I came back I had a hard time sleeping at night. Every time I closed my eyes, images of Chicago would come to my mind and keep me awake. I lived with a family there, a real middle-class family. The parents taught at the university and had two school-age children. We visited schools there, and drove around Chicago, so even though the trip was only ten or twelve days we got a feeling for the city. I was lucky because in such a short period of time I was able to go both to Denmark and to America.

What I saw in Chicago made exactly the impression on me I expected to have, corresponded exactly to what I had imagined: a very peaceful, happy way of life, with normal people able to communicate in a completely natural way. I can't say that I was awestruck, but there were things I really liked. I liked the fact that students are so relaxed and that they sit on the grass! How wonderful! I wondered, why don't students sit on lawns here? I even had an argument with a friend of mine—I told her that we should do that here, too, sit on the grass. And she went on about how in Moscow things are different, it's a different architecture, a different culture.

Now I just think of America as a different country, and one really can't say it's better here or there. It's simply a different culture, and one should relate to it calmly and normally.

Our cultures are different in every way. Friendship, for example, is very important here, but not in America. I guess that's related to the fact that Americans move around a lot from one place to another. But visiting each other constantly and spending a lot of time with friends is really important to us. And in terms of reading books and magazines, despite the negative process that's going on here now, we still read more than you do. Not everybody, of course, because unfortunately, commercialization is changing all of that. People have started reading less than they used to. Or maybe they read, but I don't consider reading a detective story the same thing as real reading. I guess you could call what's going on here "Americanization." Television has taken on more meaning, unfortunately, and it's even affected me! I hate that idiot box, but I feel like an addict. Not that I sit there for hours, but sometimes I have to force myself to get up and just turn it off. It's terrible.

After Chicago I came back here and got involved again in my cheerful university life. In my second year I fell in love with one of the women in my group, but actually we had known each other before that. In our department we have a kind of practicum—we went out to the countryside, to a village, to collect songs and fairy tales from the simple old women who live there. It was wonderful! The two of us did this work together, and it was then that we started to fall in love. And things were just great. That was in the summer, in between my first and second years. Then we came back to Moscow, and after that the two of us started traveling around, like adventurers. We went to Leningrad on the spur of the moment, not knowing where we were going to be able to stay, and then we took off for the Baltic, and ran into some people we knew there. And in the middle of all this, we had to take our exams, of course, and that's always a lot of hassle.

And then in the winter of my second year at the university, a tragedy took place. My mother died in a criminal incident. It was a year and a half ago. Naturally, that was a very heavy moment for me. Sasha, who was by then my fiancée, helped me get through that.

And now Sasha's in the hospital, under observation, because she's pregnant, and she's been having some problems. They're fairly serious problems. This is already the third time she's ended up in the hospital. They have to watch out for her, it's a critical moment. This is really difficult. We're really hoping that things will turn out all right.

So here we are, the two of us, living here in our apartment. Sasha's six years older than I am. I'm nineteen and a half. She's twenty-five. She started out studying at the Historical-

Archival Institute, but she didn't like it so she only stayed there one year, then she worked in a library, and then she went on to the university.

Last fall my sister emigrated to Israel. Three weeks ago she gave birth to a daughter. She went there by herself. Things turned out rather interestingly for her! The man she was with here in Moscow left last August for America, for Boston, to study, without knowing that my sister was going to have a baby. My sister didn't know then either. She was planning to go to Israel at the end of August, and so she left. She really likes it there. She hasn't been looking for work because of the pregnancy, but I think that even if she wanted to find a job now she probably wouldn't be able to. In that respect things in Israel are really bad. And most people who immigrate there end up cursing it for that reason. But my sister is an exception. For some reason she really likes it there. She lives in Jerusalem, right in the center. And now her young man has taken his exams and has gone to Israel to be with her. They'll probably get married now and she'll go to America with him because he has to continue his studies. When they're married she'll be able to go with him to the United States. She'll have to pay Israel back for the financial assistance given her while she's been there, but she has some friends there who have agreed to help her out with that. She won't be able to work in America, but she doesn't really want to work or stay there in any case. She wants to live in Israel. It's not that she's particularly religious or nationalistic; she simply likes Israel. She was able to adapt very quickly because while she was still here she studied the language. And also, a lot of people who go there expect things to be fine, they go there without understanding that in some ways things are even worse in Israel than they are here, but my sister was prepared. She knew the situation. And she had another reason for going. All her friends here had already left, either for Israel or for America. Almost her entire circle of friends had gone and she felt lonely here.

I wouldn't leave. I have a lot of reasons for not going. Of course I wouldn't be against going someplace else for a while, maybe to America, to study. But leave for good, no. After the death of my mother there was a moment when I felt like leaving, like dropping everything, a moment when I felt that this was a foreign country to me. But I knew that I wouldn't feel any better somewhere else. I would just be exchanging one place for another. For now I'm studying in the university and I have my friends, and of course I have to find out who I'm going to become. I don't know what will be several years from now, but at the moment things are completely fine for me here. I'm building a family life! Of course life can be very difficult here at times.

My sister had a normal life here. She didn't leave for political or economic reasons. She went because she had some kind of feeling, an inertia, a feeling that comes when all of your friends are leaving. Her life had changed a lot, and perhaps it's true that she didn't feel she had many prospects for the future here, both as far as her personal life was concerned and for her work life as well. And look, if she had had her baby here, it would have been a lot more difficult than having it in Israel! At least a person can eat decently in Israel! She has a calm life there.

And look at me! I'm paying less and less attention to the university now. All my attention goes to solving the problem of feeding my wife! It's not even really that it's a problem. It's just that your whole day goes by either looking for or thinking about where you're going to find the right kinds of food, trying to come up with some kind of idea for a meal. So of course your mood gets ruined.

PLANS

Even here, it's early for me to have gotten married and decided to become a father! People look at me and wonder! But I have a principle. I just don't believe there is one certain age—

nineteen, twenty-five, forty. I don't have the idea that I can only do this once I've done other things, that I have to do this or that first. I don't like living my life according to the Plan!

I have two more years at the university. I'm studying Russian literature, nineteenth-century. I went into the university with the idea that I wanted to get an education. I didn't know what I would do with it afterward. Of course, I would like to go on to work in the field I'm studying now at the university, but I am not at all certain that will be possible. It used to be that if a person got into the university, it was just assumed he'd go on and on, keep going in the same direction. But not now. It's not in the least bit clear what I will end up doing, concretely, later on. Maybe I'll work as a journalist, maybe I'll be able to continue at the university. I wouldn't like to get involved in what a lot of people do after finishing the Russian Department at the University—go into the schools and be a teacher. That possibility doesn't interest me very much. But I just don't know. I know that I have talents in this field, but I do have to think about earning a living, too!

Every now and then I get little part-time jobs, like translating American films. I did two films. I liked that work a lot. I'd be glad to do more. And in any case we're not going hungry. We get small student stipends, my father helps out every now and then, I get little jobs from time to time. We're managing. But we are worrying about money all the time, watching out. But that's normal for a student, isn't it? Of course I'd like to have good, serious work related to what I'm studying. I just don't know whether it will work out that way. But at the moment, in order to earn money for us to live on, I'm ready to do any work at all. Things aren't so simple now.

THE UNIVERSITY

I'm satisfied at Moscow State University. A lot depends on me, of course, but I think the classes and the professors are good. I have a very good mentor, a senior professor who has been teaching for a long time, an interesting person, a teacher with a capital "T." He really gives me a lot. And that's the most interesting thing for me. I would like more orientation toward literature than we have—it turns out that our department is oriented more toward linguistics. But I compensate for that with some special seminars and I'm basically satisfied with what I'm studying. I love to read and to write!

Unfortunately, I think the level at Moscow State is declining somewhat. The general breakdown here has reached such a profound level. It's the kind of time we're living through, a time of chaos and uncertainty. The entire old order is being destroyed, something new is being built but it doesn't exist yet, and all of this has psychological consequences. These changes aren't always good for culture as a whole, but in general I would say that the university is holding its own.

THE STATE OF THINGS

Schools in general aren't *sinking* to a very low level, they were *always* that way! But there are some very good schools developing now, with very original curricula. Of course you can count the number of those on your fingers. And when teachers start going on strike for higher pay, well . . . The schoolchildren are changing too. You can hear them. One says, "I'm Rambo." Another one says, "I'm the Terminator," "I'm a robot!" I can even see that the sixteen-year-olds in my old school are different from the way we were. Sometimes I visit my old school. Not long ago I was talking to some of my old teachers, and they were telling me that my graduating class was really the last one of the old type.

Of the kids you interviewed for the book, I would imagine that the girls are less optimistic than the boys. Women always have more conservative views than men, because, after all, for a woman, stability is very important. And in the circum-

stances this society is in, women have the greater burden,
because in most cases housework is the responsibility of the
woman. And men have more possibilities for being active. A
man always knows that so much depends on him. For example, it's not right for a man to go around complaining that
somebody is to blame for something. He knows he should be
getting down to business, because so much depends on him.
For a man, it's important to be able to fulfill himself, and his
energy goes to that. But a woman, at least in our circumstances, wants stability above all, and so she doesn't see a way
out of the situation we're in. Sociological surveys have shown
that men support this government in much greater numbers
than do women. More women say that they like the way
things were before.

My father and I had a little argument. He said he was
afraid that there would be some kind of social explosion
here, and I said to him, "No, nothing like that is going to happen here." But the worst battle that could take place here
might be a women's revolution! My father thinks things here
are a lot worse than I think they are. People here are tolerant,
they can handle it. But of course it's possible that women
won't take it anymore!

We're going through the process of commercialization
here, and even though I don't really like it, I know it's
unavoidable. Things like having more money weren't that
important in the past, but now, without more money you simply can't survive. There's also a general atmosphere of commerce that exists every place. You can see it on the street—
people are selling things, reselling things. I have an acquaintance who finished the university, a very capable young
man—he specialized in Pasternak—and they were waiting for
him to go work in the Pasternak Museum. But he didn't continue studying Pasternak; instead got involved in business,
and not the highest sort of business, either!

What's going on now is very bad for science and culture.
People going into business, or leaving the country altogether,

sometimes permanently, sometimes temporarily, to work. It's really a shame. We had some very high achievements in science and culture here, in spite of our horrible political system, but all of that is being lost now. There were good things here, too, and now, in spite of all the freedom, we're losing so many things. But I don't think it will go on this way much longer. Unless, God forbid, people's patience just runs out and things don't happen like they did last August.* Things won't go on like this. Personally, I feel skeptical about the current reforms. I don't think they're taking us in any specific direction. A lot of declarations are being made that I think are correct, and sometimes they even *do* some correct things, but there are a lot more declarations than anything else. Take privatization. In reality, there is no privatization. Gaidar's† government—well, despite all my respect for that economist, I don't know whether they're really capable of doing anything. You can talk about the example of Poland, and what they did there, or about some other countries as well, but here, really, we have a unique situation. We have a very large country—it's hard to compare it with other countries. In Poland they had shock therapy; here we have shock, but no therapy!

Still, I do support this government completely, because first of all I don't see that there is any alternative, anything better than what we have now. And also, this might in fact be the type of government that with time could actually end up doing something, come up with some real reforms. But for now, well, look, prices have gone up, prices have been freed, and that's good; but it has to be connected with some real reforms in production, and so far that hasn't happened. Of

---

*Ilya is referring to the August 1991 coup, and people's determination to defeat it by taking to the streets and erecting barricades.

†Yegor Gaidar, a young economist and an important member of Yeltsin's administration, is known as the chief architect of Yeltsin's initial economic reform program. He became a target of widespread criticism and, under pressure from the parliament, was eventually demoted from his position as acting prime minister.

course, they say they're doing that, but up to now they haven't. Probably they need time. It's normal for production to fall in the first stage of reform. That's what happened in Poland.

The government is responsible for a great part of the problems. For example, taxes. They've raised taxes so high that production just isn't developing. It simply isn't profitable to open up a business. The goals are right, but they have to take some very specific measures. The most important thing, of course, is privatization. Right now they privatize a factory as a formality, but in reality the same monopolists control it, even though on paper it's been privatized.

The price rises in January were really a shock. But the terrible thing is that this "January" just keeps going. Things are going up and up. You can take it for a while, a month, three months. But now, according calculations by the International Monetary Fund, inflation is at 1,000 percent! And things could get worse!

THE COUP AND THE BREAKUP OF THE UNION

During the coup in August we were at the dacha. The night before the coup we had been sitting up with some friends, and, by chance, we were talking about things. For some reason I was in bad spirits. All of my optimism had left me, and I was cursing, saying how terrible things were, how awful it all was. In the morning our friend had to leave early to get to work, and he woke us up. So I said, "Seryozha, really, why are you doing this? Why did you have to wake us up so early?" And he said, "Listen, do you remember what we were talking about last night? Well, they've gotten rid of Gorbachev!" And I said, "Stop joking, it's not April Fool's Day!" But then we turned on the television and saw that it was true. Of course my mood really got low at first, even though at the same time I had the feeling that none of it was very serious. During the first hours of the coup I thought, "This can't last for long."

So Sasha and I went into Moscow from the dacha and in the subway I saw leaflets with Yeltsin's call to resist—they were stuck on the walls with wheat paste. Sasha and I and my father all went to this huge meeting in front of the White House. But people weren't really all that upset. In the bus I even heard some people saying, well, that's what they needed to do with that Gorbachev!

The worst part of it was that night when they shot those three young men.* There was this feeling that something terrible might happen. I said to Sasha, "Get out of here, go home," but she wouldn't. They were saying that some soldiers were on Yeltsin's side, but it was hard to figure out what was going on.

About the Soviet Union breaking up, I suppose on the one hand it sounds bad—after all, Europe is uniting and here we are, splitting up. If you look at it in the abstract, from the outside, of course, it is too bad. But the situation we had here, that kind of reality, well I think that the breakup is natural. The hope that something would change had already passed.

I think the students at the university care less about these things than they did when you were here. Three years ago was the time of newspapers, magazines, rallies, and demonstrations. And now it's just the opposite. There's a real depoliticization now. And it's not that things are quieter, it's just that people are fed up with talking about these things.

Many students have just gotten involved with commercial matters—buying, reselling, that kind of thing. We have a bulletin board in our wing at school that's just full of advertisements that say I'm selling this, I'm buying that, etc. But I can say that even three years ago, students were not the most politicized element in society. They were active, of course,

---

*Three young men were killed during the popular demonstrations in defense of the government immediately following the coup, although not all three of them died by gunfire.

but most of the activity was from people older than students—my parents' generation. My father, for example, continues to be as politically active as he was then. Of course,
some people have become disappointed.

It seems to me that the best thing a person who supports
this government can do at the moment is simply to endure a
while longer. That is, the most progressive position to take at
this point is to not be against this government, rather to just
wait it out, have faith that something better will come. There
are times, of course, situations, in which one wants to get out
there and take a stand to support this government. For example, after the last Congress of Deputies here, we were ready
to get out there and defend the government. But even that's
gotten more difficult now, because the reforms are really not
popular at the moment. It's not even so much that people are
against the reforms as they are simply against the high prices!
The material situation isn't even at the level it was at the
beginning of perestroika. All the effort it takes to feed yourself, well, everybody has really grown tired. It's true that people are eating less than before. I can say that from my own
experience. Little by little you get used to less. Somewhere
along the way the standard became a different one. But all
these things will pass.

As far as freedom is concerned, at least I can say that I am
not limited in any way by anything. And as far as political
parties, please! There are about eight hundred of them now
in Russia. And some are important. I think our political life is
going well enough. There are lots of newspapers, things like
that. But of course there are economic problems, and full
political freedom has an effect on the economic situation.
Now there's been a wave of strikes—miners, doctors, teachers,
and so on. When the Moscow Emergency Services announ-
ced that they were going on strike, my father was against it.
He said, "Well it's true that I earn very little, but I know that
the government doesn't have very much money, and that's
why I'm prepared to accept what I make."

Three years ago I was very full of hope. I think I didn't understand the difference between glasnost—freedom of speech—and freedom in general. Freedom in general happened after the coup, without a doubt. Up to that moment things were still very much under the control of the Communist Party, which was preventing the reforms from being carried out. I started saying that things were fine here too early, before they really were. But I'm not a pessimist now.

MARRIAGE AND FATHERHOOD

Sasha is an apolitical person. She says, "Well, I don't really understand those things." Politics doesn't interest her very much. But that could be because at the moment, everything that has to do with the stores and the prices has fallen on my shoulders! Of course, every now and then I tell her some astronomical figure, so she knows how much things cost, but still, I'm the one who does all the shopping now. And the cooking. Of course at first we divided things up, in half, but I was always the one to always do the shopping. The cooking, cleaning—we split those things.

Patriarchal ideas are one thing, but as it turns out, Sasha is the kind of person—well, she made me understand, and in general I agree, that it's hard for women to make the rounds of stores, because after all, a woman is weaker than a man. But it's hard for me to judge these things at the moment, because really we haven't lived together that long yet, and now Sasha is expecting a child and having complications, so of course all of this has to be on my shoulders. We'll see how things turn out later.

At first I just felt neutral about having a child. I thought, "Well, having a child *now*?" But I can't say that I had this attitude that everything has to be according to a plan, at the right time. Sometimes I did mention that to Sasha, about the right time, and so forth, but I didn't have a firm idea that life goes according to the Plan. And then I started to like the idea.

Sasha really wanted to have a child, very strongly. At first I was afraid, but I think anyone would be afraid. After all, I'm only nineteen, how am I going to provide for a child? But eventually I realized that I just had to have a calm, natural attitude toward it, and now that's the way I feel.

But of course, a lot of people are saying, "What, have a child now? That's terrible, in these conditions!" But if you sit around and think like that, then in our country it's likely that nobody would have a kid for the next thirty years! And unfortunately, that tendency already exists—in Moscow the mortality rate now exceeds the birthrate. Births have dropped quite a bit. I think my father probably thought that it was early for me to be having a child. Anybody would have thought that! I had those thoughts myself. Here I am, still a student in my third year and already having a child!

"BOMZH": NO FIXED ADDRESS

MAXIM

Eighteen years old, trained as a chef,
currently unemployed

It is only through luck that I am able to find Maxim. He has no fixed address, no one place where I can get in touch with him. I call the communal apartment where his parents and sisters live, but the man who answers is not a relative and is rather unfriendly. He tells me that the family is not there and will not be back for weeks. I have the telephone number of Maxim's grandmother, which he gave me three years ago, but nobody answers when I call. Finally, I run into a young man who knows Maxim, and although he has not seen him in a long time, he assures me that he will find him. Rumor has it, this young man tells me, that Maxim no longer lives with his grandmother and has moved in with a "friend"–he uses the feminine noun ending deliberately, and smiles.

During the last days of my trip, this young man comes through on his promise: Maxim calls and later appears at my door. He has grown solid, quite tall, over six feet, and looks older than his eighteen years. His smile is kind, and he strikes me as a pleasant and attractive young man. As we talk he is serious and respectful and expresses himself with much greater ease than he did three years ago. Yet when I ask him about the specifics of his current situation, his answers are vague. He tells me that he has left his grandmother's apartment, but when I ask him where he lives, he waves his hands as if it's not something he really wants to discuss. "At some friends'

MAXIM

house," he answers, using the third-person plural, deliberately non-committal. I don't press the issue. But for one whose living and work situation is so unsettled, Maxim seems remarkably at ease, self-confident and unworried.

After I finished the culinary course at the Hotel Moscow, I took a work assignment there for one year. Afterward I was planning to get into a technical school to finish my secondary education. The school's program was related to what I had already studied in the culinary course. So I got all my papers together to enroll, but then I took a vacation in the south and by the time I got back, the exams were over and I had missed my chance that year to get in. So instead I went to work for the Ministry of Supply and Deliveries as a cook in their cafeteria. There was a cafeteria there, a sort of buffet, for all the bosses who worked there. Downstairs at the ministry the café was pretty plain, but upstairs, where the bosses ate, it was better. I worked upstairs! And it seemed that they ordered completely different food in the two cafeterias. They served cutlets in both places, but they added a lot less bread to the cutlets upstairs! Secrets of a Soviet chef!

I liked working there at the Hotel Moscow. I liked the work and the collective. And the restaurant itself was pretty good. They use good food products there, it's clean, really nice. But then I transferred over to the Supply Ministry, and I didn't like working there. They had everything you could want, but I couldn't have any of it! They had good brands of cigarettes, German beer, but all of that went to the bosses, I couldn't buy any of those things for myself. Maybe once a week I could buy a pack of cigarettes. They had those things lying around by the crateful, but they sold it only at the special buffets. And the highest salary you could make there was 90 or 100 rubles. The Hotel Moscow paid twice as much, and you could buy all kinds of things at the buffets there.

When I left my job at the Supply Ministry, I went to work at a security company—the kind of place that provides guards for offices and places like that. I had about half a year left before I was supposed to report for military service, so I worked as a guard and then left because I was called into the army. The half-year flew by so quickly. I had wanted to go into the army, but that's not how it turned out. Right before I was supposed to go report for duty I had to go into the hospital, so when they called me up that's where I was, by coincidence. I had been getting ready to go to Poland on a trip. I was supposed to catch an evening train, but that morning I was shopping in a store and suddenly I started to feel bad. My blood pressure went way up. So they called an ambulance and took me to the hospital. Later they said it was something that happens to people my age. And as it turns out there were a bunch of young men in the hospital resting quite comfortably in the same room with me! They didn't want to go into the army and that's why they were there. They convinced me to try to get out of it, so I decided to try. It's not even that I had a strong desire not to go into the army. I just wanted to try and see if I could get out of it. They say it's not realistic to think you're going to pull one over on the doctors without bribes or something like that, just by fooling them. Sometimes young men do fool them, they end up in the hospital, but by the time they're out of there they really *are* sick! But in my case, it turned out that I was able to fool them, without bribes or anything. They would ask me what hurt and I would tell them I wasn't sure, that I was gripped by fear and felt weak. The thing is that I did once I have a concussion, a long time ago, and that's written in my medical records. So I told them that during sports practice I had had a second concussion, I just didn't have the medical certificate where it had been recorded. And so they released me from service and said that I had a nervous condition. I have a certificate that says I only have to serve during wartime. If we're at peace, I don't have to serve. If there was a war, they could call me.

But I'll tell you, I regret not having gone to the army. Things have more direction there. You get up in the morning and you know where you're going to go and what you're going to do there. I think everybody should go to the army. At least try it. I think I would be a different person now if I had gone into the army. There's a kind of discipline in the army, especially in the navy. It's most desirable to go into the navy. They have discipline there. And when you go out on a ship, you get to interact with the outside world for half a year.

I don't think I would have lost two years. You get training in the army. You learn things, if you want to. A guy who wants to practice sports, for example, can train in that sport for two years. You have a lot of free time there, and each person can study what he wants to. But not everywhere of course, it depends upon where you end up serving.

THE CURRENT SITUATION

Things really fell apart quickly here. We were one country, and in the course of a year the whole thing fell apart and people started talking about all their differences. And all these shortages that appeared. It's gotten much harder to live because of perestroika.

Things could have been done differently under perestroika. More intelligently. More attention could have been paid to the different nationalities and to developing their cultures, their nationalism, on a more rational level—language, culture—but not to the extent that they've done it now, and without letting happen what has already happened, the wars, secessions. All of this has started now. It wasn't like this before. But it's going to stay this way. Pretty soon everybody is going to be asking for their independence.

Things are simply a mess right now. Everybody is trying to find a way to make a little bit of money in order to survive. They try to steal something here and there, in order to sell it. Prices go up but wages don't, and some people are really on the verge of death. Look at the pensioners. They're going hungry. You can see it on the streets—women over seventy years old, begging, selling things. They got used to living under Stalin and they can't forget that. They still respect him, even now. You'll never convince them about what's going on today! They're doing everything they can just to find empty bottles they can exchange for full ones they can sell on the street, for a little extra money. And they're not doing it just to make some money, they're doing it in order to stay alive.

PLANS

I haven't worked since I got the draft form back with the medical exemption. For almost a whole year I haven't worked. I'm not really doing anything. It would have been harder not to have a job before perestroika, but as it is, because of my age, it's not looked on too badly as long as you don't get into any trouble, you don't end up at the police, get caught hanging out, doing something. There are still laws against parasitism but nobody is going to enforce them. You can see the militia going after drunks on the street, with their megaphones, and when they stop them they ask for their papers, and whether they have jobs. But if you go around normally and don't get into trouble, nobody's going to go after you.

I don't know what I'm going to do after this summer. I'll make up my mind. Maybe I'll go back to work. I left my last job because I didn't like the place. They asked me to go back to the ministry, and the Moscow Restaurant at the hotel is also inviting me to go back, but for now I don't want to. I don't know that I want to be a cook anymore. I don't really know what I want to do.

I don't want to get involved with all this selling and reselling for higher prices. It's not even real business, just speculation. I don't think that's right. I can understand people who produce things themselves, but there aren't very many people who do that anymore, produce things and sell them, and get money for that. Most people who are selling are selling things they bought and then get more money for them. There's no control over the people who are selling on the street. Not unless you're in a market or someplace where you have to pay somebody for your stall. And the racketeers who control all of that are like pimps.

So with the way things are now, I wouldn't like to try to open up my own business. Not unless it was somehow in the area of agriculture. Far away, and where you could really have a lot of land, because you need a lot of land to get results. Agriculture is really important right now. When I was a child I spent a lot of time in the Caucasus, with one of my grandmothers. There were horses there, and ever since then I've loved taking care of horses. If you have that in you from the time you're a child, it doesn't go away. I know how to take care of horses, look after them. I know how to ride—I spent a lot of time doing that. It was easy there, because there was a horse farm nearby. Of course I don't have the chance to do that now, but maybe someday I will.

Or maybe I'll open up my own place to sell things like bread. It's easy to bake your own bread and sell it. So what if it costs a ruble more than in a state store, it's always warm, and fresh. And so you get a profit and people are satisfied.

I can't really say that there have been any changes for my family, but I don't spend that much time with them right now since I don't live at home. They're living more or less the way they were. Things are more expensive, but their salaries have gone up, too. They don't have a lot, but they have enough. And this year they are supposed to be getting an apartment. Three years have gone by and they still don't have one. But they should, this year because now they're a "family with many children" since my other sister was born, and because they've been waiting ten years for an apartment. I have another little sister, Vika, who is two years old, or a little less. Actually I don't know exactly how old she is now, that's how infrequently I see my family.

My parents have actually been offered several apartments but there was always something wrong with them. Either the building was too old and in bad shape, or the apartment was too small.

I was living with my grandmother before, but then my cousin got married and my grandmother gave my cousin her apartment, and she went to live with her sister. So now I'm living with a friend. So I'm really a *BOMZH**—I don't have any one place to live. And I'm unemployed too.

PERSONAL CHANGES

My view of the world has changed. My view of everything around me. Before, things seemed so easy to me, things seemed good, I saw good in everything. And in the last three years my views have really changed because I see that everything is not that easy, everything is not that good. I've changed in a spiritual sense, too—that is, those qualities like kindness, faithfulness, and honesty. I haven't found myself yet though. I wish I could find the one thing that I could do with pleasure. The kind of work. I would like to go to an evening technical school to finish my secondary education.

I don't have any ideas yet about my future family. It's still early. Actually, I almost did get married last year. But thank God I didn't, I saved myself from that.

I'd still like to see some other country, since it's easy now. I might be able to go to Poland this summer, by invitation. I could work there, in a restaurant, maybe as a chef. Maybe I'll work in my profession after all.

---

*The Russian acronym for "without a fixed place of residence" (*bez opredelennogo mesta zhitel′stva*).

"I WANT TO STUDY"

YELENA

Nineteen years old, clerical worker and typing/computer data entry instructor at a production training center

I see the domestic side of Yelena first: the blazer and skirt she has sewn, the bakery-perfect marble cake she has made for our meeting, the way she sits, legs crossed, hands neatly folded in her lap, her delicate smile. She is gentle but not reserved. In a quiet tone she tells me about her work, which she likes, and about her family's life, which has become more difficult. She takes a bite of cake from time to time, lifts her teacup from the saucer, takes small sips.

The quiet mood is broken when she begins to talk about her greatest desire at the moment–to enter the university. She explains why she has not been able to, tells me what is lacking in her education, what has kept her back. Her words now come swiftly, in measure with her great disappointment. But Yelena is determined. Somehow she will get her education.

She calls me a few days later, uncomfortable and apologetic, to tell me that it she will not be able to meet me over the weekend, as we had planned. Coincidentally, I learn from a friend of Yelena's that colleagues from work have invited her for a weekend of canoeing and camping. When I do see her again she is tanned, relaxed, happy. She never does tell me that she canceled our meeting for a weekend in the woods.

After I finished school I tried to get into the History Department at the Lenin Pedagogical Institute—now they call it the

YELENA

Pedagogical University. I took all the exams, but I was one point short and I wasn't accepted. So in the fall I went to work at a production training center where students in the upper grades get their work training.* We work with computers. The first year I was a secretary there and all my work was secretarial. Now I'm working as a master† of production instruction. That means I guide the students through their practicum, I teach them how to type and how to work on a computer. For the most part the students are girls, but there are some young men too.

Then, the next year, I again tried to get into the Pedagogical Institute, in the Psychology Department. But I didn't even get through the first exam, which was biology. That's as far as I got. I wasn't prepared. And after that I tried to get into a polygraphic institute, but that—well, that was a step that came from desperation, just to get in anyplace to study. But thank God I wasn't accepted there either! I really couldn't have studied there. That's not for me. But I thought I just had to get in to study someplace.

And this year I want to get accepted somewhere. I know I really want to get an education, but I can't say exactly what it is I want to do. I know that I want to be accepted in some institution of higher education and then be able to work in the specialization that I study. My goal right now is to get a well-rounded education. I'd like to master as much science as possible. History. Literature. Maybe journalism. Languages. That's why this year I want to try to get into the university, into the History Department, to learn history, which I have

---

*Students who remain in the academic track typically have weekly classes of some type of work-related training during their last years in secondary school. In Yelena's case, she learned how to type and how to enter data into a computer.

†"Master" is the title of nonacademic instructors in vocational and technical-training institutes. A master has expertise in the particular area in which he or she teaches but does not have to have any pedagogical training.

always found very interesting. Then I would like to study English. I would like to work as a translator and guide. Or maybe just a translator. So at the moment I can't say that I have one particular goal. I would like to study several different professions, and I'd like them all to be interesting to me. I would like to study different things.

The problem is that our educational system is monolithic. It has no flexibility at all. To get what you really want, what's interesting to you, from one of our institutes of higher education is really complicated. We have one fixed curriculum, with a list of courses you absolutely must study. Even though I don't know exactly what I want to study, I have to choose one institute and try to get accepted there, and take the courses they prescribe. But I've heard that there are some institutes now that are creating their own system of studying and are more flexible and more interesting.

I'm still interested in teaching. In fact, what I'm doing now can really be called teaching, and I find it very interesting! But I wouldn't want to work in schools the way they are now. They're very underdeveloped. We have a primitive system of education. If I could change it, come up with my own curriculum, my own way of teaching, and not have to follow the same system that exists now for every school, then I would like to work as a teacher.

Our system is primitive in the sense that when a child finishes school now, secondary education, he doesn't really know any single one of the subjects he studied very well. He doesn't even have an average level—not in history, not in languages, not in literature—unless he goes to a special school.

I know I'm lacking a lot of knowledge! When I tried to get into the institute I could really tell. But I'm not blaming anybody for that. I have the chance now to study those things by myself and get the knowledge I need by myself. Whether or not I get accepted someplace now depends only on me.

WORKING

I ended up at the job I have now completely by accident. I'm there just because it's the same place where I did my own practicum when I was a student. I went back and they offered me the job. And in general I'm not sorry, because I really do like it there. I teach typing and how to use computers.

I can't really say what my salary is, because it's supposed to be going up now. Who knows what it will be? But before this it was around 900 a month because I was still a secretary half-time. It all goes together—a master, full-time, plus half-time as a secretary, and also some additional pay for the harmful effect of working with computers—magnetic fields all the time, so they pay me extra. Really, what I earn isn't even the minimum needed to get by. But I do get by. I don't have a family of my own, and I'm the only child in my family. Of course it's a low level of getting by! My salary is so low because I can't work as a teacher officially, since I don't have the education. So I'm only a master, and therefore I get a lower salary.

Working is completely different from being a student. I have a work collective and everybody there is over thirty, forty. Of course it's a completely different way of communicating, and I'm much more responsible for what I'm doing than I was in school. In school you don't feel any responsibility for yourself and what you're doing. But once you go to work, you get that feeling very quickly.

I can't say I'm sorry that school is over for me, but I do regret that I haven't been able to continue studying. I would like to work and study at the same time.

FAMILY LIFE

My father just opened up his own business. He's one of the founders of that business. It's at the same place he worked before, at the radio and television factory. He makes televisions. There's a business concern called Rossiya that rented one of the divisions at the factory, the division in which they make televisions. And in that division, the workers organized a small business. They rented it.

There isn't really a big difference between the salary he was getting then and what he's getting now. In my family we hardly ever talk about the way things are now, so it's hard for me to say what it's like for him. I know what his situation at work is, but as for how he relates to his situation, well, I don't know. My father would like to do something at work, on his own. But his mood is not that pessimistic. Perhaps because my parents never really did relate to their work in a certain way, it never really did give them any kind of spiritual satisfaction. Maybe that's why. But now he has the opportunity to open up his own business, to do something, and I think he likes that. The founders of this business are my father and his friends and this business concern, Rossiya. Rossiya finances the business.

My mother is still working where she was before. So my parents are still working together at the same place, but now they are in different divisions.

I can't say that my family's standard of living has changed that much, although I can say that all of my parents' salary is spent on food. Together the two of them earn an average of about 4,000 rubles a month. Most of that goes for food. Other things have gone up, too—the telephone, the apartment. We feel the difference. We can't allow ourselves to buy things we might have bought before, or to take a trip somewhere the way we could before. In fact, taking a trip anyplace is just impossible now, whether to some other city or even to a cheap vacation home someplace. The three of us together don't earn enough to take even one trip! A trip now costs up to 10,000 rubles. The last time we took a trip somewhere was a long time ago. And even then we took the cheapest kind of trip available, to a tourist station. When I traveled a lot, it was with school groups.

We've started eating less than we used to. We don't eat fruit anymore. And not all vegetables, certainly not in the quantity one wants to buy them. We're lacking vitamins! If you have to choose, people prefer to buy a kilo of meat rather than a kilo of tomatoes. And that's terrible, for people who have kids. You have to raise them to be healthy, but it's too hard now. It's hard to get dairy products, and kids need them. You have to stand in long lines, and they're not always available. You have to be there right when they make the deliveries. They bring the milk, and in two hours there's none left. In spite of the fact that prices are so high! Even bread has gotten so expensive, 7 rubles a loaf. And if it's been awhile since there was a delivery to the bakery, there's always a line, and some kind of fight going on there.

And now there's a new problem related to food. With such high prices, a lot of food just spoils because it doesn't get sold. It's too expensive, it doesn't get sold on time—eggs, for example—and it wasn't even brought to the store in the best of conditions. Then people eat it, and there's been a lot of food poisoning.

I don't talk with my parents about what's going on here. I prefer not to talk to them about it. It's just that their point of view about these things is quite different from mine. I try to judge the situation objectively. I don't say "All the democrats are bad, and the Partycrats are all good. When they were in power at least we had something. Then the democrats came to power and now everything is bad, and we should stand them all against a wall and shoot them." Of course I can't say things like that. I'm trying to be objective about everything that's going on here, but my parents aren't able to. I think that often they blame the democrats for everything that has happened. They feel pretty negatively about what has happened here in this country.

I think the reason why people are standing for all of this is because the change hasn't been so drastic. It's not the case that yesterday we had everything, a hundred times more than now. In our view, as far back as we can remember, something was always missing. There were always problems with something—getting an apartment, or a dacha, or a car, then with food, especially later on, and with things, clothes. There have always been problems. That's why we can take this, why someone from outside, like you, might come here and think, "How in the world is it possible to live like this?" But as horrible as it seems, we've gotten used to it. Maybe it's even good that we have this characteristic, this patience. We have different views of life from yours. Knowing what we know about America only from television programs and from the stories of people who have been to America or the West, well, it sounds crazy to us when you tell us that your economy is weak now and that there has been a kind of recession. To say that in America right now there is an economic slump! That sounds wild! I suppose you look at that from the inside and have your own view, but for us, well, we have different ways of measuring that. We probably have never had the chance to develop the same kinds of demands as you have.

It's clear that right now our life is complicated in terms of our economic situation. If I do have my own family, I'll try to do everything to ensure that this difficult economic, material situation does not affect my family. Right now that's such a problem in many families. This constant irritation, this lack of satisfaction really spills over onto the family life. There is a lot of negative energy collecting in people, and it gets taken out on the family. I'll try my hardest not to let this happen to my family. Even if there will be material difficulties, no matter what, they shouldn't have an effect on my relationships to people and on people's relationships to me. So fine, let's say there are going to be impossible prices. That shouldn't be a reason for me to be in a bad mood, to make me bitter in relationship to what surrounds me. I think any situation has its solution. Even if I have don't have a kopeck, that doesn't give me the right to take it out on other people and start making demands on other people.

I know a lot of people at work who are going around in such a defeated, heavy state, who feel that they have lost the meaning of life. For the most part they are people who have been working for years, older people, and the way things are now just doesn't fit into their thinking. They've spent their whole lives working, and now all of a sudden they're beggars and they can't allow themselves to buy anything.

That's why I think my life will be difficult, but still, my relationships should be all right. It's so important to maintain good human relationships and to keep some kind of warmth in the family. Not to bring all the dirt from the street into the home. In fact, just the opposite, the dirtier it is outside, the cleaner things should be in the home and in one's surroundings. Because in the final analysis, all these material things are not the most important ones.

In these times you have a choice: you either think about ways you can make money, get into business, or you think about spiritual, educational, not material things. One or the other. If you get 900 rubles a month for your work, you just decide you're going to live without a dacha and without a car. Period.

POLITICAL CHANGES

I thought positively about Yeltsin three years ago because then, when everything was still just beginning, we could compare him to what had gone on before him. And then it seemed to us that Yeltsin, as an alternative, as head of the government, would be able to do something. It seemed that way, from the way he talked.

But what were the first things he did? He banned the Communist Party. That was a completely senseless thing to do. Useless. There was a need for some concrete deeds. And what does he do? Bans the Communist Party. And in banning the Party, Yeltsin used the same methods that were being used before. That is, the method of prohibition, exclusion of certain ideas or theories. The same way the Bolsheviks at the beginning of Soviet power destroyed their political opponents. This is just the same thing—the destruction of your opponents in order to hold on to power.

In general people should be able to relate to their government with respect and with trust, and the government should treat people with respect. And right now there isn't any of that. I think the current government is trying to resolve its own political problems, its own struggle for power. And some of the speeches they publish in the newspapers, all over the country, for everybody to read—how can you respect some of that nonsense? I think you can see that they're missing something, intellectually.

And you know, I do think that in fact, some of those socialist ideas are really very good ones. How to plan a more just life through union . . .

MARRIAGE

Well, my search is under way! So far I haven't met the kind of person with whom I would like to link my fate, but that doesn't keep me from looking! I can't say that I'm not worried about it at all. But I can definitely say that my future life's companion is not within my current circle of friends and colleagues. I think I'll know when I do meet that person. Sooner or later, but everything comes in its due time.

I think what's going on with me now is normal. I don't have the feeling that I'm lonely. But even that feeling of loneliness for a certain period is normal. A person has to go through that so that later on she's able to evaluate a relationship. It's normal to learn from your experience. You don't have to accept it quietly. I know of several girls who went ahead and got married because they were worried they weren't going to meet anybody else. That happens a lot among people our age. They're scared. And that's related to the question of women's psychological dependence on men.

A lot of men here don't respect women. It's a lack in their upbringing, since all that comes from the earliest childhood. On any bus you can see a boy—let's say about five years old, I consider that's already fairly grown—and this boy should stand up and give a woman his seat on the bus. Maybe it will be hard on him, but a woman who's working has it even harder. This kind of respect for women has to be developed in them from childhood. A young boy should notice if his mother or grandmother doesn't feel very well, he should be aware of it. But that doesn't happen around here very much. And that's why so many young men here grow up to be selfish and they don't notice what's going on around them. They start to think that it's their due to have a woman hovering around them, doing everything for them, working like a servant. And they don't have the slightest feeling that that isn't right and that they ought to help out. And all of this comes because of their relationship to their mothers and grandmothers when they're little boys. They get used to everything being done for them. And they transfer this feeling to their wife, to their girlfriend, this exact kind of relationship. And it gets hard to correct it in yourself, to get to the point where you realize that it's wrong.

"THE ARMY WAS REALLY AN IMPORTANT SCHOOL FOR ME"

DIMA

Twenty-one years old, vocational school graduate, living in Canada

I have a Canadian address in rural Ontario from a card Dima sent me months ago. But he has lived on several farms, and by the time I call Dima has already moved on. After a number of calls to different families I learn that Dima and his friends have gone to live in Toronto. Eventually I get his current phone number. One of Dima's roommates answers with a very Russian version of "hello." The roommate calls Dima to the phone, and I try to imagine the house they're living in and how a group of young men from Moscow find living on their own in Toronto. When I ask Dima, he says "It's wonderful." A superb city, he adds.

During our conversation Dima reminds me of the expense of a long distance call–he's worried about my phone bill! "I'll write you everything," he promises. But I want to stay on the line a little longer. I ask him if he's changed. "I'm a lot taller," he says with a laugh. "I don't think you'd recognize me." His voice is deep. He sounds like an adult. I ask him about his plans. Will he be staying in Toronto? But the question makes him uncomfortable. His reply is vague and I do not understand what he tells me. He ends the conversation with another promise to write about everything. I hang up feeling troubled, as if something went wrong at the end of the call.

DIMA

*Within two weeks time a letter arrives–twenty pages long and
very thorough. I am surprised by how quickly, and how much,
Dima has written. He tells me the story of the last three years with
careful, writerly attention to the selection of detail.*

*His letter reveals why he could not answer my question about his
future. This is a difficult moment for Dima.*

FROM A LETTER FROM TORONTO

In June [1989] they took me into the army, one day after my
eighteenth birthday. A lot of my friends from school and
from the chorus* saw me off, and a lot of my relatives, too.
We spent the whole night at my house, it was a very noisy and
cheerful party! All of us guys from the chorus went out onto
my balcony and sang our songs. It was so nice, people from
neighboring apartments who still hadn't gone to sleep came
out onto their balconies and listened to our singing. When we
were finished all the people on their balconies gave us a big
round of applause and asked us to keep singing. I think we
were singing so loud that even those who had already gone to
sleep woke up and were listening to the Russian Folk Chorus!
But somebody must not have liked it because two policemen
showed up at our door and we had to end our concert!

I ended up serving right next to our border with Poland,
in a very special unit: anti-aircraft defense. Our task was to
monitor carefully the air space of the Soviet Union and of
four neighboring countries—Poland, Hungary, Czechoslovakia, and Romania. My specialization was called a "radio-location station operator." This is a very interesting and demand-
ing specialization that carries a lot of responsibility and

---

*Dima is referring to the amateur chorus, run by the Ministry of Voca-
tional Education, in which he, Lyosha, and Alexei participated at the time
of the 1989 interviews. It was through this choir that Dima and Lyosha
became involved with the youth center in Moscow that sponsors the agricultural program they joined.

requires a soldier's attention. We monitored the movements of aircraft on a radar screen.

Once I reported that our station was ready and operating, I received instructions and directions from the commander. For example, one task consisted of detecting and keeping track of the airplane carrying the president of the USSR, M.S. Gorbachev, flying on some official visit. We had to be able to report very precisely all of the coordinates and the exact location of his airplane and guide it through the air corridor between the border of the USSR and beyond. Or, for example, we had to detect any airplane that illegally crossed our border. Usually I would give the coordinates of the aircraft to our pursuit planes and they would find it, make contact with it, and force it to land at the nearest airport, or send it back across the border. It depended on the seriousness of the matter, but basically they were just small agricultural aircraft that were working the fields and constantly keeping us from getting any rest or peace.

I remember one funny incident that happened to me in the army. Once, in the summer, when the harvest was in full swing, I was sent by my commanders on a trip to a city right on the border, where I was supposed to take part in some training exercises for a week. And on one of those hot days I was on duty with my partner. He was sitting at the screen and I was free, so I was reading a book. Suddenly he screamed at me, "Dima! Call the command post as quickly as you can! They're trying to attack our border!" Naturally I didn't believe him. So I went up to the screen and I saw that the screen really had picked up three aircraft flying very slowly toward our border. Accordingly, I began to follow all the instructions I had from above. I called the operating guard at the command post and let him know that we had detected three unidentified objects. They were exactly three kilometers from our border, and so the operating guard took decisive action: he called for a state of first alert. All the guys who had been relaxing dropped whatever it was they had been doing and ran the kilometer and a half to their work posts in five minutes. Everybody was waiting for further orders and waiting to see what was going to happen next. Everybody was thinking that there was going to be some kind of attack on the Soviet border! Then the operating guard sent me to the observation tower, from which you can see everything. He gave me binoculars and the task of detecting exactly when those airplanes appeared. Then I was supposed to report immediately to the command post what kind of airplanes or helicopters they were, where they were flying, and for what reason. So of course I immediately ran to the post and climbed up and searched the sky quite diligently and at length for those aircraft through a pair of binoculars. Meanwhile, the operator at the screen watched those objects flying right up to the border! The commander at the command post was completely beside himself! They kept calling me and asking, "Well, what do you see?" And I had to answer, "There *isn't* anything out there that I can see, and the sky is clear!" Then they really started getting even more worried. The airplanes were crossing the border, everybody was running around, going crazy, but still I couldn't see anything. I was starting to think that maybe we were hallucinating from such unrelenting work with no breaks. And then suddenly I saw them! They appeared! And I almost fell from that height to the field below, I just couldn't believe my eyes! From behind a small hill three combines appeared, harvesting wheat! I've never laughed so much in my life! I called the commander by phone at that point, but I couldn't stop laughing. Everybody thought I had lost my mind. But then I ran over to where everybody was and I told them what I had seen, and of course after that they all started to laugh, too!

Everybody remembered that story for a long time! There are a lot more incidents I remember, but there's not enough paper to tell you about them all. I could be a lot more detailed about the life of a soldier in the army!

Every morning we got up at six. The sergeant major would

head over to the barracks and shout, "Company! Time to get up!" At the sound of that command blankets would start flying up from the upper bunks to the ceiling, and still-sleeping soldiers would start falling down from the bunks to the floor! From the outside, this must have looked very funny, seeing as everybody's eyes were still closed and everybody was still finishing up their dreams. From sheer rote memory all of us would start to get dressed, still in such a sleepy state that they would grab other people's things and start dressing in whatever came their way. For example, they'd button their tunics all wrong or put their boots on the wrong feet or their caps on backward. It was pretty funny to watch!

After that everybody would go outside and leave the people on duty in the barracks to straighten the place out. All the rest would run to the morning exercises. They let us wear sneakers instead of our boots, which I did. I'd go running three or four kilometers with a friend of mine who loved a healthy lifestyle as much as I did. It's really beautiful when you go running on a road through fields and in front of you the sun is coming up. After the morning cross-country we would usually do exercises on a horizontal bar and on other gymnastic apparatus. We'd do different exercises for about forty-five minutes. After that we'd go get washed. In the summer they'd put up basins outside and in the winter inside. We'd get breakfast at seven. All the soldiers would line up on the drill grounds, and the sergeant major would walk through and inspect each soldier, how his hair was clipped, his boots shined, was his uniform clean? Whoever had any mistakes wouldn't go to breakfast but instead would have to go correct the mistakes. That happened to me a couple of times, but I got out of the situation quickly enough. I'd run back to the barracks and take things from friends who were either on duty or who were ill and still lying in bed, and I'd confidently head over to the dining hall.

We'd have a light breakfast, hot cereal and tea with little open-faced sandwiches. Of course you can't fill up on that!

Then we'd all go outside again, and the assistant commander of political affairs would hold classes where he'd go over political information. At those classes the only thing everybody wanted to do was sleep. Usually they would tell us about all kinds of world affairs and how the plenary sessions of the Central Committee had gone. That ended at eight o'clock, and then all the soldiers, the whole battalion, would go on out to the most important mission of the day: the roster of military duties. That's a very ceremonious lineup of all the soldiers and officers to receive orders and report for their next twenty-four-hour duties.

We would all line up in rows so that the commander could see each one of his soldiers. The leader of each division would approach the commander and announce its readiness for the day's work. The commander would receive the reports, make decisions, and make some announcements or clarifications. Then he'd read out the day's orders, and they'd play the national anthem of the USSR as they raised the flag. As the anthem ended the whole group would turn and march ceremoniously past the flags. The trucks that would take us to our positions would drive up.

We'd get to our station and relieve our guys who had been on night duty. Our shift was from 8:30 A.M. to 2:00 P.M. If our station wasn't operating at the moment, if the screen wasn't on, we'd take the time to check and make sure everything was in working order and we'd fix any details that weren't right. When our station wasn't in operation, another station in another city would be working. At an agreed-upon time they'd turn off their station and we would begin working immediately.

It was hard work once that screen went on. Somehow you just didn't feel like yourself, looking at that screen, especially during the day. Fifty to sixty airplanes flying within a radius of 400 kilometers! We would only give information for an area of 250 kilometers, about thirty-five airplanes at once, and you have to remember them all and transmit that and

not get them confused or you can end up completely wreck-
ing all that military work.

I can tell you from my own experience that this is really
difficult work and at times we would get very tired. Our turn
at the screen would last for three or four hours, and you
would divide it in half, evenly with your partner. To do that
whole shift by yourself would be the equivalent of having
somebody make off with half your health and half your nervous system! An untrained person simply wouldn't be able to
take that kind of psychological or physical pressure. He'd
look at those thirty to thirty-five planes in one spot, how they
move around, fly close together, separate and then fly off in
different directions, and he wouldn't be able to do a thing,
the way I couldn't during my first days.

The commercial passenger flights are very easy once
you've learned their flight paths, but the most difficult are
the military planes because they fly any way they want to. If
they feel like it they change their speed, the direction of their
flight, and their altitude. You have to pay special attention to
them.

But finally the long-awaited hour, two o'clock, would arrive
and we'd be relieved by another shift of our guys. One would
take my place, and I'd pass on exactly all the information I
had. It takes a memory in good working order to do that! So
they would work and we would go back for lunch.

We had good lunches and good cooks, young women who
really tried hard to cook well, and they did. After lunch, at
three, we had lineup. The commander would make some
small announcements and whoever was going to be on night
duty would be released to go rest. And everyone else would
either do some kinds of jobs or go to classes. But my friend
Kostya, whom I always spent time with, and I would go get
some sleep until evening. Kostya was also from Moscow and
we became really good friends, and in difficult moments we
would really stand by each other. He is a really good person,
very cheerful and always ready to make a joke, which is of no

small importance in the army when you really need a break in any spare moment you get.

We'd sleep from three until seven, then go to supper, and then it would be our turn to work again. At night things would grow quiet and all the planes and pilots would take rests. Then it would get completely peaceful—only one or two planes flying, sometimes none at all. And then we would be able to relax a little bit. We'd sit around and talk about things, we'd remember Moscow and how good things were before we went into the army, when we did whatever we wanted and we were absolutely free. And we didn't have to get up so early! When we would just spend our time with friends, or fishing. I did the things I liked best then! And we'd dream about that long-awaited day when we'd return home to our parents and friends.

I ended up thinking about a lot of things when I was in the army, about what I would like to get a chance to do in life, and I came to some conclusions about what I had accomplished so far in life and how much I had changed during the time I served in the army. Perhaps I started to relate to work in a much more serious way, and to behave myself as a member of a large collective in such a way that people in the collective would care about me and respect me. The army was really an important school for me. I learned how to overcome obstacles and difficulties. I had to become accustomed to the fact that for two years I wouldn't have any of the people I was close to near me. Who could imagine how a soldier in the army waits for a letter from home or from his beloved girlfriend? Or how happy soldiers are when they get these letters? Nothing can lift a soldier's spirit like a letter from home.

In our battalion there was a very large collective of different nationalities, guys from all the republics* and from some other countries as well, and everybody got along very well.

---

*The other republics that, along with Russia, made up the Soviet Union.

We were one collective. And we didn't have any of those interethnic conflicts that were taking place at that time in the USSR. We knew that if we allowed any conflicts to take place on the basis of nationality, that one national group or another would take up arms. Of course there were some small incidents, but the guys would argue and then resolve their conflict in a friendly way.

But when I first went into the army in 1989, the situation there was sort of heavy in some ways. Some of the soldiers who had already served their year and a half or their two years loved to make fun of the young soldiers. They loved to humiliate them to their faces and in front of their buddies. They would make the young soldiers work for them. And if one of the younger guys stopped listening to them, they would beat him till he was bloody. But after they all finished their service and went home we were able to change things somewhat, to make sure that our guys wouldn't end up going home as invalids but rather would go home healthy, strong, and in good shape.

During my service I ended up making three trips through the Soviet Union. In the summer of 1990 we were sent to the city of Baku. That's in Azerbaijan, where there's a real war going on now. That was just at the time after that night in Baku when people's blood had been spilled. It was dangerous to go there. We went to Baku carrying a secret cargo—a radio-location station—and we were given arms to defend it. But we went in an ordinary freight car used for all different kinds of cargo. We traveled for ten days. It was very interesting to live in those conditions. We cooked for ourselves. The whole time we stood guard over our cargo with automatic weapons. There had been many incidents in which young guys like ourselves had been attacked and had their weapons taken from them and were killed. But thank God everything went fine with us; nobody attacked us and we all made it back. After that I made two more trips, and then I got a leave to go home, because of my good service. When I got home nobody was there and I ended up sitting and waiting for someone to get home from work! After about ten minutes my mother came home, and was she ever happy to see me!

That was in January, just after the New Year. I met up with all my friends and went to rehearsals of the chorus. I just hung out and had a good time and got a rest from that military service! I was in Moscow for two weeks and then I went back to the army, but I knew that in three or four months I would get to go back home for good. I was really pleased by the fact that I would be going home during the nicest time of year—summer—and that I would be able to celebrate my twentieth birthday not in the army but at home, at the dacha, together with my buddies.

I was released from the army on May 12, and I went home. I felt like I was the happiest person on earth at that moment. All of that was behind me, and now I could become a normal person again. After a week in Moscow, around the first of June, I left the city and went to the dacha to help my parents. After the way I worked in the army, the work on the dacha seemed to be just sheer pleasure! Digging in the garden or collecting berries from the bushes. But of course I wanted to spend time with my buddies, since I hadn't seen them in two years. They were happy to see me, too, and asked me all kinds of questions. They found it interesting because many of them hadn't gone into the army.

During the day I worked in the garden or helped my father build a garage. And in the evenings we all gathered around a campfire in the woods, played the guitar, and would stay there until five or six in the morning. Then we'd go home and sleep until noon. It's too hot to work during the day in the summer. Sometimes a group of us guys would get together and go to a huge lake called Senezh. We'd take boats and go swimming right in the middle of the lake. The water in that lake was amazingly clean and there are a lot of fish. I love going fishing, and while I was at the dacha I never missed the opportunity to go with my friend Dimitrii and my brother Sergei to catch fish.

I became interested in a project to get agriculture back on its feet again. Young people who were interested were invited to go to Canada to live with farmers and learn about their life and their work.

I flew to Canada on September 8, 1991. There were four of us who went. We flew to Montreal and were greeted there by farmers who took us out to their farms. They were French. It was the first time in my life that I had any contact with French people. They were a very interesting family, with a dairy farm. They made cheese. We worked at their farm for one month and then we were taken to Ontario, to a farm about 150 kilometers from Toronto. We stayed with a farmer who had two huge farms. Two of us went to live with him, and two of us went a little bit further on, to the neighboring farm.

We started working there from the first day. We got up at 6:30 A.M. and went to the morning milking. We milked the owner's cows and we helped him feed the other cows, clean them, and a bunch of other tasks. The farm was very clean and comfortable and completely automated. After the milking we'd have breakfast. After that we'd go feed the cows and then work in the fields. We helped build an electric fence, and we planted trees around the edges of the fields so that later on, when they grow, they'll protect the fields from the wind. After we worked we'd have lunch at noon and then we'd get two hours of free time. We'd relax or listen to music or we'd get on our bikes and take a ride to see our guys down the road.

We'd work again until six and then have supper and do the evening milking. I'd bale out hay and straw for the cows and calves. Lyosha would go to the next barn and feed the veal calves and the beef cattle. Then he'd come help me. The farmer finished the milking, and we'd all go clean up and go home. Sometimes in the evenings, too, we'd ride our bikes to visit our friends.

One of the farmers there directed a Bach choir and he'd take us to rehearsals. We really enjoyed that, and then we'd stay for a while and walk around that town. Sometimes they'd have birthday parties and we'd be invited and we'd have a good time. When winter arrived it was time to go, so we asked them to extend our visas, which they did, willingly. We stayed another three months. I moved on to another farm and spent the rest of the time there. It was a small farm, only sixteen dairy cows, for cream. The whole farm had twenty-five pigs, a lot of chickens for laying eggs, three horses, and all the rest of the cows were for beef. Lyosha went back to Montreal when his visa ran out, and he flew back to Moscow.

The problem with the program was that we needed to be on those farms all year. Especially in the summer. But the way it turned out we didn't see the harvest. The program picked a bad time to send us there because we didn't get to work in the fields.

When I go back to Russia I'd like to be able to work in agriculture. I joined the farm project because it seemed new, interesting, and because it's really important to raise the level of agriculture in Russia. There's too little being produced there, and it's too full of chemicals. But I don't want to go back to Russia right now. In fact, after we worked six months on the farm we went to visit some friends in Toronto and decided to stay there and see what would happen. We lived in their basement. We fixed it up ourselves. Summer came and we started to like it even more around here. This is a beautiful city, green, and not at all like Moscow. We spent the summer walking around, swimming, getting tan. We went to visit some acquaintances to go fishing—they have a very beautiful lake.

In July we rented the house where we're living now. We live in the center of Toronto, a very convenient area. There's a metro station right next to our building. In September I'd like to start studying English and see if I can get into college. I like Canada and I'd like to stay here for awhile.

I've started going to a Russian Orthodox Church. People should have some kind of faith in their lives. It helps a person get through. And it helps people deal with the end of life. I didn't want to tell you about this over the phone. While I've been here in Canada a very sorrowful thing happened. My father died in Moscow. This happened in April, but my mother first wrote me about it three weeks ago. She told me that he went with some close friends of his to work on the dacha. And at night the dacha burned down, and they burned with it. By the time the firemen showed up, it was already too late. And it was too late to call me back to Moscow.

I think you probably understand my situation and the situation of my family. Now I am the only person who can help them, and I can only do it from here. There's nothing in Moscow, and they don't have enough money because we don't have my father anymore. And I am the oldest and I have to find some money. The material level in Russia is really bad. Prices are high and things are scarce. My family is counting on me now. I don't have any other solution.

BECOMING A FARMER

LYOSHA

Twenty-one years old, vocational-school graduate, trying to become an independent small farmer

I meet Lyosha near the monument on Pushkin Square. He has grown, is over six feet now, and I am shocked by the difference between the gangly teenager I remember and the tall young man approaching me. At first glance he looks much older. But as we begin to talk I realize that he is much the same: still shy, still hesitant and careful when he talks, a little embarrassed by his own words yet trying hard to find a way to make sure I understand the details of what he is telling me, particularly when it involves specialized terms he assumes I will not understand. He is patient, even when I need a third explanation of the same thing within no more than ten minutes. He knows a few farming words in English from his stay in Canada and tries them out on me, blushing.

Lyosha is dressed in a handsome light wool jacket and fancy trousers, and has a well-styled haircut; he seems to be just as careful about his appearance as he was three years ago.

The day before you left Moscow [in 1989] was the day I was called up into the army. I went to a place about a thousand kilometers to the southeast of Moscow and was there for half a year in basic training. We learned how you're supposed to march, how to salute, but actually I was doing that for only three months. And then for the other three months I was in the hospital. I was sent home early from the army for med-

LYOSHA

ical reasons. I told the doctors I was having severe back pains, like I had kidney problems. I poked my finger with a needle and put blood in the urine samples. That makes it seem as if there is some protein in the urine. And that indicates that the kidneys are not working. The hard part was doing those things in such a way that the doctors wouldn't notice what I was up to.

The thing is our doctors have really poor equipment, so they couldn't prove whether the pain was real or not. They try to figure it out, but it they can't always prove it. They know that a lot of guys are just faking it, and a lot of guys don't pull it off, but I got lucky. They believed me. I complained a lot about serious pain.

I don't think anybody wants to be in the army. Everybody tries to do something. But half the guys who try to do something aren't able to pull it off. Of course I had to be very clever and really work at it! I can't even tell you all the things I did. Maybe your doctors in America can make a definitive analysis, but not here! Maybe in Moscow, in central cities, but not where I was in the provinces! Those doctors try to figure out who's fooling them and who's not, but they can't always do it!

After I got out of the army I went home and for three months I just took it easy, resting at home. After that I went to work at a factory, in my profession, assembling radios. The factory was near where I live, but it was really an unhealthy place and I didn't want to keep working there. You work with tiny pieces and there's a lot of smoke and it's bad for your eyes. I worked there for a month but I couldn't take it so I left. I don't like that profession. That's clear.

Next I worked in a cooperative, doing something with eyeglasses. Then I went with the chorus* to America, to the state of Oklahoma.

---

*The amateur Russian Folk Chorus, in which Dima and Alexei also participated.

I had imagined America differently. I probably thought that the colors there were different from the colors here, but when I got there I saw the same colors as here. And people, the same. When you look at American films, all the colors are so bright, so beautiful. But when you get there, it doesn't look the way it does in a film. The colors aren't quite as bright and beautiful! They must make those films look a little better!

America changed me. I don't smoke anymore. I was living with a family and they really got after me for smoking! So I promised them that when I got back to the Soviet Union I wouldn't smoke anymore, and so I came here and stopped! And I don't think so much anymore about how to dress or how to find nice clothes. I think I started looking at things in a different way. I have different conversations now. I don't know exactly how to describe this. I look at things more simply now. Not just clothes. Other things too.

When I came back from America I started to work again, for about a year, in the cooperative with some friends. And then the farmer's project appeared, at the center* I was work-ing in. There was a German who came and started to talk to us about the farming project, and it seemed interesting to me so I went to Canada, for the experience. I went there in Sep-tember, and we lived there with the farmers and helped them out. I was there for three months.

Of course, by the time we got to Canada, most of the farm work was already done. We were there in the "dead season." There wasn't much to do in October, November. We did some things, worked on the natural fertilizers, helped with the animals. I worked on two farms, a dairy farm and a beef farm. We helped out but we couldn't stay in winter because they didn't need any more help then so they couldn't put us

---

*Lyosha began doing some part-time work at the youth center that is sponsoring the agricultural project before he actually became involved in the project.

up. When I returned to Moscow I took courses in farming for two months at the Timiryazev Agricultural Academy, and then I got going with the piece of land they gave me.

The project is having a lot of problems right now. You can rent land long-term, but you can't sell it. In other words, you can work the land, but you can't buy it and resell it. You have to produce something on it. So, let's suppose a person has bought land and he's put some money into it, let's say he's built a house, but he doesn't produce anything for a couple of years—actually I think it's three years without producing. If they come by and find out that nothing is being produced, the land will be confiscated. The government will pay you back what you put into it. I don't like that. Suppose I have a bad harvest or the weather is bad or something for a couple of years. They'll just come and take the land away.

The sponsor* of the project provided the capital for renting the land and gave credit for the technology and houses. But of course up till now it's just been words. He's just gotten the land now. There aren't any houses there yet, and only two tractors, and they're still not in working condition. So far I've plowed up as much as I could with a spade! So I'll only have some things for myself, some vegetables, some potatoes, onions, tomatoes, cucumbers, just like having a small garden plot. But really I'm supposed to have thirty hectares there. That's a lot of land. The land belongs to the center, but I will have the right to buy it out over the course of several years. I'll be buying the land from the center. But for now the center is just leasing the land, and if the project doesn't work, they'll have to give it back. So if they give us three years to produce something, one has already gone by, and we might not get the crop in this year either.

---

*A wealthy Soviet émigré now living in Western Europe provided the youth center with the funds to start the agricultural project. Many new entrepreneurial projects depend upon private sponsors, and the concept has become so important that the English word "sponsor" has been adopted into the Russian language.

You see, the center leased the land from a state farm. The director will be keeping an eye on us, and if he sees that we can't get the project going, we'll lose the land. Things are terribly complicated. When the state farm gave the land, the director promised to help, to give us tractors. All kinds of promises were made, but so far there hasn't been any real help. They're tricking us. They don't want to help. And the problem is the state farm. The center gave the state farm half a million in credit for the land, but they're not fulfilling their part of it.

For example, the director of the state farm promised to give us a tractor, and we asked him about this every morning. We would go to him and ask about the tractor, and every day he'd say, "Tomorrow, tomorrow, tomorrow." For two weeks in a row he kept saying "Tomorrow." That was about two or three weeks ago. Now a month has gone by and nothing has been plowed! The people from the center went to talk to him, and he promised them to do it, but when they leave, he doesn't do anything.

I was waiting for them to bring a battery for the tractor from Leningrad on Sunday. Actually they were supposed to deliver the battery along with the tractor, and the tractor came two weeks ago, but the battery's just arrived! So the tractor was useless for two weeks. And it's still not ready! It needs a special kind of water that gives off a current, so we need this water, and we still don't have it. All this was supposed to be ready weeks ago. And with the tractor there was supposed to be a plow, and there was also supposed to be a cultivator. They brought one plow and that was it. It's really sad. I don't get it. They just don't let people get down to work. I know a lot of farmers, and they all have problems. They give them land, so they buy cattle, and they promise to give them hay, promise they'll help them with everything, but they don't do it. They don't give them anything!

I know one farmer, well, I wouldn't exactly call him successful, but at least you could say he's getting something done. But the state farm never comes through with its promises to him. They give him problems. Now he's being forced to kill off some of his cattle because he doesn't have anything to feed them. He has only a small piece of land so he can't grow everything he needs to feed them. And he's got to break even. So if he kills half of his cattle, he can survive. But then he's only got a few cattle left, and he really needs to have more to make ends meet. The directors of these state farms just don't want to lose their power. You see, if a farmer is well organized, he can produce twice as much as the director of the state farm, even though the state farm may have six times as much land. A farmer who works well will be much more productive and get much better harvests than the state farm, and the directors are jealous of that. And they want control because they're used to it. For sixty years, they've been the most important ones. So I think they do a lot of these things on purpose, to keep farmers from being successful. Of course, that system is going to have to break down, but I think it will be a long time yet before that happens.

When you saw me two weeks ago my mood was more optimistic because there was still time to plant then. But you see this is the last week, really, when it's possible to do the plowing and planting of large areas of land. They promised that everything was going to be ready by last week, but it wasn't true. The time has gone by in these weeks and I don't think I'll be able to get a large crop into the ground now. The most important questions have to be resolved this week. I can't wait too long.

For now I'm living with my mother and father, and my mother isn't working, she's got a health problem. So if the problems aren't resolved in the next two weeks, well, I have to help my family, bring in some money. My family is just barely surviving now. We have enough money to pay for food and that's it. That's one reason why I really have to start earning something now. I eat at home, so I get by. But my stipend from the center is only 600 rubles. That's really nothing. I

may just have to go find a job someplace. I'll probably go to
work in a store or something, as a salesman, because the
salaries are pretty good there. That's why I would go. So I
may have to leave the farmer's project, if it seems that there
are no prospects for getting the work done. Because you see,
if I stay in the project and we can't get a crop going for this
year, then I am going to spend a whole year with nothing—no
money, and nothing to do.

But I've taken some courses in farming, learned to drive a
tractor, to weld. How to plant, prepare a crop. The various
aspects of farming—plowing, planting, learning the equipment. So I've studied this stuff! But nobody is allowing it to
happen!

Three of our guys are still in Canada. They're supposed to
return and get involved in the project, if they don't change
their minds! If they come back they are supposed to get land
in the same place I did, 120 kilometers south of Moscow.
There are two farmers helping us, one from Spain and one
from Germany, and they have a car, so they take us back and
forth. But they're living in tents out there because they
haven't built the houses yet. We're actually supposed to be
meeting at the center later on today to discuss the problems,
because the Spaniard and the German aren't very happy with
the way things are going either.

They're part of this movement of Rudolf Steiner, a German who was interested in farming only by natural methods.
They don't use nitrates, fertilizers, they don't use tractors!
They plow with horses. Of course we're not going to plow
with horses! But our harvest is going to be ecological, without any chemicals. It'll be clean. Their system uses biodynam-
ics, it's bio-organic, that's how they harvest and grow their
crops. Bio-organic is different from just organic. Organic
means just the way they're raised, no fertilizers, only manure,
but bio-organic means actually making compost using certain
kinds of flowers, oak bark, many different kinds of mixtures.
They're very complicated because they have to be prepared

according to the stars, according to certain times of the month. A certain star is out, or the moon in a certain position, and all of that affects plants in different ways, and they pay attention to all of that. At first when I heard about it I laughed, but when I saw the results that they get! I ate a carrot that I had never tasted before in my life, juicy and sweet, like I had never seen. They make their mixtures at night. Depending upon the light of the moon, the rays have a certain effect. I laughed, but I started to believe in the system because I saw the results.

I really want to be able to continue with the project. In the meantime I will continue to live in the city, but if we can get things going out there and build houses, I'd like to go live there.

THE PTU

I'm not satisfied with my decision to leave school and go into a PTU, even though I was satisfied three years ago. I would be able to "see the light," get out of my darkness, if I had finished school. There are a lot more opportunities if you've finished school. It's easier with a good education. You can get a well-paid job or continue studying.

It's true that you get a profession from a PTU, and if you just finish academic secondary school you don't. But I think that if I had kept going in school and graduated, I probably would have gone on to an institute. That's the way most people do it. If you finish tenth grade, more than half of those people go on to an institute. They go right after school. They don't just go straight to work.

But I don't think I'll try to get into an institute now. It's too late. I don't know enough. I haven't studied for four years already. Maybe it would be worth it to try, I don't know. I'm scared to do that. I suppose I could really sit down and prepare myself, study hard, but I don't know if I have the patience to do it. I'm not certain that I could. But I haven't

even been thinking about that. I've been so involved in the
farming project that I'm just not thinking about that now, and
I'll go on with the project unless I realize that it's
useless . . .

If I had finished school it would be easier to get into an
institute, but four years have gone by and my brain isn't func-
tioning anymore. Mathematics, physics . . . I suppose I have
some confidence in myself, I have a good memory, I have the
ability to study, but I'm a little afraid.

As far as academic education goes, you don't really get
enough in a PTU. If you study in a PTU it's easier. There's
less work. They demand less of you. The way I remember myself at the time I made the decision, I was capable but lazy.
That's why I was attracted to the PTU, because you see the
way it is if you go there. If you study, you study, if you don't,
you don't. If you show up or you don't, it doesn't matter.

We didn't really study there. I don't know how to say this,
but it's hard for me now to find some way to converse with
the guys I know who finished the PTU with me. They don't
have an intellect.

I can say that if I had to make the decision again, I
wouldn't do that. But at fifteen, you don't listen to what people tell you.

GOING INTO BUSINESS

ALEXEI

Twenty years old, co-owner of a small optical cooperative

It takes Alexei a while to warm up to me. When I first call him he does not seem at all surprised to hear from me, nor is he particularly friendly. He responds to my voice so nonchalantly that it seems as if we spoke no more than a week ago. But he does agree to meet me in a few days at Pushkin Square, at eleven in the morning.

He arrives more than an hour late, nervous and agitated, explaining that some urgent business delayed him. He looks around the square repeatedly. He is waiting for someone else who is supposed to meet him there—someone connected with his optical business. We wait for this person for another half an hour, but finally Alexei gives up and I suggest that we go for lunch at the McDonald's on the other side of Tverskaya—formerly Gorky—Street. Alexei says that it is the easiest place to have lunch; since it has become so expensive, the lines to get in are much shorter now. But he will not accept my invitation to buy him lunch, and he orders only a black coffee. As we sit he talks a little about his optical cooperative. The conversation seems stiff and distanced. Alexei is restless, clearly has something on his mind. After no more than twenty minutes it is already time for him to go. Urgent business matters, he says.

The second time we meet he comes to the apartment where I am staying. It is midafternoon and he seems more relaxed. I watch and listen to him carefully, trying to gain an understanding of the ways he has changed over the last three years. But today he seems like the eager, younger Alexei of three years ago, full of stories and anecdotes. He tells me emphatically that he still cares about making a

141

ALEXEI

fashion statement, asks me about Suzanne Vega's third album, wondering if I could get it for him. He tells me that he is hurt and upset because a young friend he made from the United States has stopped writing to him and he cannot understand why. He relates the story of how he just spent 1500 rubles to buy some sacks of sugar so that his family will be able to make preserves this summer.

He drinks the tea I serve, eats generous portions of cheese, wheat crackers, raisin loaf. He rummages through his backpack and shows me some of the lenses he uses to make his eyeglasses. The afternoon turns into evening; Alexei is in no hurry today.

I can't say that I really finished the PTU, I just disappeared toward the end. When the time came to take my final exams, I didn't even prepare for them because I knew that no matter what, I didn't plan to work in that field, even though the PTU had already selected a work assignment for me. I was indifferent about the whole thing. I thought to myself, "To hell with these final exams!" I showed up in shorts and an old t-shirt and told them that I hadn't prepared anything! They gave everybody 3s and 4s. They gave me a 4, like everybody else, so there wouldn't be a scene. I was very relaxed about the whole thing. They gave me a 4 just for showing up. So I have the diploma. Big deal, so they gave me a grade of "good" instead of "excellent" because I told them that I hadn't prepared anything and I wasn't about to do anything! And then I promised each one of the examiners a bottle of cognac as I was leaving. But I forgot about that cognac, I didn't have any money at that time anyhow.

They sent me to work at a construction site, with another friend of mine, Misha. They sent us to a state farm, *Moskovski,* where they grow a lot of greens, tomatoes, vegetables. We were supposed to work on a building there. But they didn't give us work in our profession.* Instead they sent us

---

*Carpentry.

out into the fields, into the heat. They said to us, "Guys, we want you to go out there, somewhere within a kilometer there is a telephone cable. We'd like you to go out and look for it. Dig for it. Find it." So we asked, "How are we going to find it? Where is it?" And they said, "We don't know. Go and look for it. If you find it, you find it, if you don't, you don't. But we know it's there. A secret cable, a military cable. They forgot about it a long time ago and that's why we don't know where it is. Go ahead and dig for it. Let us know if you find it." So we dug, for about two months. Of course I can't say we did a lot of digging. It was hot, and we were too lazy to dig, we'd keep going off and eating cucumbers and tomatoes, but really we had no choice but to go out and dig at least a bit. They really didn't know where that cable was, and they had to lay out a whole irrigation system in those fields, without knowing where that telephone cable was. They knew only that it was there. And they couldn't lay in the irrigation system until they knew where the telephone cable was, because they could have broken it. And it was a secret telephone cable, out to Vnukovo airport. We were supposed to find it, neatly, carefully, so it wouldn't get broken. But of course we didn't find it.

We dug for two months, and then I started getting ready to go to Greece.* I went up to the boss and I said, "You know what boss? I have to go on urgent business to Greece." And he said, "What are you talking about, going away? You're not going anywhere. You're going to stay here and work at your job!" And so I said to him, "This isn't my work! My specialization is not in digging!" And he said, "True, but with time we'll find you work in your field." I said, "Well, I'm going." And he threatened me with legal action, if I left. I turned my back on him and left. And I didn't show up again. My friend left, too.

---

*The Russian Folk Chorus started to receive invitations to give concerts abroad around 1988–89. Alexei was able to go on trips to Greece and to the United States as a member of the chorus.

And so then I went to Greece with the chorus. Greece is so beautiful! The most beautiful country in the world!

When I came back I thought, well I have to go to work someplace. I looked around and then I found a place in a fire fighter's brigade. I went there, and ended up working nine months. I had to get up in the middle of the night, be ready to go out to a fire anytime it was necessary. Even on my birthday, only one month after I had started working there, I ended up going to put out a fire, a car was burning on a highway. And I went there, soaking, it was raining, and there was a problem and I came within a second of burning up. I was saved by half a meter, half a second. And so I started to think, why do I want a job like this? But I worked after that another eight months, and then I ran away from that job and decided to get into commerce. And I've been working in commerce since last August.

I had some acquaintances who worked with a group of opticians, with some other guys, and they were hardly earning anything. They had a miserably poor little cooperative, they earned almost nothing. All of them were ready to leave that cooperative, to shut it down. And so they gave me their booth. They asked me if I wanted to work there, so I said yes, I wanted to. They told me that if I wanted to work there, I would get 50 rubles a day. I thought, well well, 50 rubles a day, what a lot of money! I said, of course! And I went to work there, at that optician's. And Misha, the guy who worked with me digging for the cable, went to work with me, too, but he didn't like it. It wasn't a lot of money for him. So I was left there working by myself. When I started working there, nobody else was really doing anything. After one week working there I could see they were doing things wrong. They only sold glasses that were already assembled, bad glasses, ugly glasses, nobody was buying them. So I wrote an announcement that I was fitting lenses. I went and ordered some lenses. In one day I would fit from two to four lenses into frames. And I would get 2,000 rubles a day into my pocket! I worked

for more than a month. I was able to get the lenses from
other people who already had them. I made order forms,
receipts. I made my connections, found a technician who
would fit the glasses for me. It got to the point where I had to
pay about 200 rubles a day to get somebody to help me get
the work done there. Now I'm paying people 500. I don't really know how much I make there.

I started working there right around the time of the coup,
the first day after the coup. I work there every day, including
Saturdays and Sundays. There hasn't been a single day since
then that I haven't worked. So really, it's as if I've been working there three years already! But I like the work. I like making glasses. It satisfies me. It's not hard labor. You don't have
to make a special effort. I take the order, for whatever lens is
needed. I select the proper correction, get the order filled,
and that's that. I don't make the glasses myself. I see if I have
that particular lens, and I go to the technician, I pay him, and
he fills the order for me.

It's a very rare kind of business, and one that really pays
off. Because I can get not just 15 percent a day, like other
businesses, but 800 percent. Just for one order! Because I
have rare lenses, the kinds that are hard to get, and if cus-
tomers go to another optician to get it done, it can take a
month. But I fill the order in one day. And that's why my
optician's store is really pretty popular.

But there have been problems. After I had been working
there for a while and things were going well, the friend who
invited me to work there said, "Look, I want you to leave.
We'll divide everything up in half." But I had already put out
advertisements, I had paid my share, but he still wanted me
to leave. So I said, "All right, I'll go." So I spent a while wondering what to do. And then I said to myself, "Go ahead! I'll
open up my own little business." I hooked up with some of
my old friends and went in with them. We thought this out,
went out into the streets, went out with out advertisements,
just when private commerce was first allowed. I still had my

reserves, after all, the eyeglasses, and we went out and sold them. It turned out pretty well. We made some money working that way for two months. Out in the cold, in February, in the coldest time! But we earned enough money to open our own little business, rent a space, and that's where I'm working now.

I'm not really sure how much I'm earning a month. Maybe about 3,000 rubles, more or less. It's still not clear. After all, we've only been working there about two months. But I'm having problems again. When I first opened up the business some people said to me, "Don't bring your friends there to work with you. They'll end up taking advantage of you. In two months they'll start thinking, why should he be here? Once you let them in on all your secrets, give them your contacts, when you let them know how to organize everything they need to do, they're not going to need you anymore. They'll be able to work alone, without you." And that's the way it turned out. It turned out to be the truth! They're already saying to me, "Go on, you can leave, we don't need you anymore!" That's what they're saying to me. Of course it's my business, but they've already started to take it into their own hands. They don't need me anymore, they can already do everything by themselves, without me. I gave them all my contacts, all my connections, told them about all the different ways to solve problems, and now they're in the position to say to me, quite calmly, "Alexei, get out of here, leave the business."

Just about two weeks ago they took the document that shows it's my business. They were on the way to finalize our lease on the booth, so they took the document with them and they haven't brought it back. I don't know where the document is anymore. They kept it. I didn't pay enough attention! And so they staged a coup on me!

I may have to leave. But I'm going to try to keep on doing the same work, open up another optician's shop, only this time without any "co-founders." In some other place. Of

course I'm in a very tense situation right now, but I always
have been! I've never had a moment that wasn't full of ten-
sion. If I have to leave this business now, I'm going to find a
way to borrow 50,000 rubles in order to open up the same
kind of business again, my own this time! To open up a business costs about 35,000 right now. Just to rent a booth costs
15,000 a month. So I need about 50,000 rubles in order to
really get down to business. I already have all the papers I
need to open the business but I need 50,000 to get started.
But I don't really have any place to get those 50,000 right
now because I've drifted away from all my contacts lately. You
see, I borrowed money to open up the business I've still got
with my two friends, and now I'm the one who has to pay it
back. The other two guys are just saying, "Well you're the one
who borrowed it, so you're the one who has to pay it back!"

I don't have any training as an optician. There is special
training for opticians, but it's at a very low level, the level of
the PTU, and what they teach you to do there is only to set
the lenses into the frames. Unless you go into medicine, at
the level of higher education. But that's not for me. I'm getting my education from life, and I must say that as far as the
work of opticians goes, I know what I'm doing more than a
lot of trained opticians. And what I do is really useful for
society. It's priceless! I give people their eyesight! I get them
glasses, so they can read, work. If somebody's glasses break,
he might have to wait for a month to get them fixed, and he
can't read, he can't work. But I can get him his glasses in a
day!

I don't think I could find better work than what I'm doing
now! I like being able to give people their eyesight! Imagine,
if you need lenses that are minus ten, twelve, fifteen, it's just
impossible to get your hands on them in Moscow! But I have
the connections and I can get them the glasses in the course
of one day. For people that is simply such great happiness
that they say they're ready to pay any amount of money! And
I get to name my own prices!

don't have connections, you'll never find lenses. I got these contacts because I became acquainted with various opticians. I met some opticians and they introduced me to other ones, and they introduced me to a third group, who introduced me to a fourth one who told me about the channels I need in order to get the lenses. All these shortages we've had around here with lenses all these years have been false shortages.* It turns out there are a lot of lenses around here. When you were here, three years ago, there were great deliveries of lenses from Germany. Look, I can even show you some of them. But people couldn't get their hands on them. They cost me 8 rubles when I got them! And now I sell them for 500! They're the remains of the humanitarian aid we got here. There were tremendous reserves of them, but you couldn't find them, because they were all held by the Fourth Department†—you know, the Communist Party. But they were here! And these are the last bits of those shipments and I've just started to get them because I have an acquaintance who worked in the Fourth Department, some people I met when I was working on Gorbachev's dacha. Did I tell you about that?

I worked on Gorbachev's dacha more than a year and a half ago. I've lived about four lives since you were here! I was still studying and was supposed to be assigned a practicum, and they asked the PTU to select some of the best students. For some reason, out of that whole bunch I was chosen, and

---

*Eyeglasses have always been a particularly difficult item to find. Available eyeglasses were known for their lack of stylishness, and it was common to try to get eyeglasses from other countries in the former socialist bloc that had better-developed light industry, such as Czechoslovakia.

†The Ministry of Health was divided into four departments. The Fourth Department was responsible for providing services to members of government institutions such as the Supreme Soviet, the Central Committee, and so on. Thus the expression "the Fourth Department" when used in conversation often carries a sense of irony because of the obvious privileged status and superior quality of services that it implies.

a friend of mine, Misha. They selected us for a practicum at a closed site. The only people who worked there were soldiers and the KGB, and we ended up with the KGB. They took us to Gorbachev's dacha, near Moscow State University. And there it was, one of the "green dachas"* right next to the one that was Stalin's dacha. A five-story dacha. For some reason they came to our PTU and asked for two carpenters, for some reason they didn't have any there in the KGB. So they sent us there, to work on the moldings between the floor and the wall. Their moldings were really complicated, from Austria, because the dacha had been built with such expensive materials, the walls, two rooms for showing films, long halls, probably about twenty rooms on each floor! Our government certainly lives better than we do!

Across the fence from us we could see a hospital belonging to the Fourth Department, a hospital for the Central Committee. And we were supposed to lay in a long pipe through there, and because of that we were able to get into their cafeteria to eat. We would eat in that cafeteria—you should have seen it! For 1 ruble and 40 kopecks I was able to really fill my stomach, like I had spent 150! They were selling real delicatessen. Olives, for 3 rubles a jar. I bought so many of them! Every day I would buy and bring home several jars, half of my refrigerator was full of olives! I still have some left.

Everything there was cheap. The hospital was just fantastic, nothing compared to the usual hospitals we have. It was a sanatorium in comparison, everything clean, quiet. It was hard to get into the cafeteria, but they just mistook us for workers who were working right there and they let us in. And did we eat well while we were there! And practically free, 1 ruble 40! And such big portions, a normal person couldn't eat them. We would eat them between the two of us! We were

---

*The reference to the color green comes from the tall fences, painted green, that hid the luxurious dachas of government officials from public view.

sad when we left that work site, because we had been able to eat so well there.

I'm not interested in getting a higher education. When I told you three years ago that I was, I wasn't, really. Or maybe then I was thinking, "Well, perhaps, maybe I'll still get a higher education." Or I thought that when I grew up I might want to go onto an institution of higher education. Well, I've grown up now, and I see that I don't want to!

To tell you the truth, I don't really imagine my future anymore. Or maybe I imagine it this way: I'll sign some kind of agreement with somebody in Poland, I'll get selling rights to things that have gone out of fashion, that already aren't in demand anymore, things that stores haven't been selling for two or three years. You see, our fashion here is about five years behind. In Poland those things have already gotten very cheap because they're not in demand, so I can make good money off of them here!

But really, I'd rather keep doing what I'm doing than just make money off of selling things at higher prices. I've had a lot of offers to get involved in deals where I could make a lot of money. In ginseng for example. There are certain channels where I could buy it, and then there are some channels I could use in order to process it, get a hold of the equipment to process it, to granulize it, and then sell it for fantastic sums, ten or twenty times more, because buying it unprocessed is cheap, but in granulated form it is much more expensive. So I had the chance to do that. But really, I've gotten used to working at my optician's booth, and I like doing that. I'd like to keep on doing it. I usually work from ten in the morning to eleven at night. I don't have time anymore for my old hobbies like folk music and the chorus.

I never used to pay attention to people's glasses before. I just wasn't interested in that, what kind of correction, what kind of lens. Now I've gotten so involved with glasses that when I walk down the street and see a person, I look at his glasses and I know what kind they are and how much they cost. I remember every pair of glasses I made! I can go up to somebody and say, "I'm the person who made your glasses!" I like what I'm doing. I like working as an optician. I tried so many things! I even tried selling things, cigarettes. I bought them and sold them at a higher price. Salems, Marlboros.

I make a lot of money! If I were working alone, didn't have those "co-founders" who have started dictating their conditions to me, I could earn up to 100,000 rubles a month! I'm sure of that! I think that the problem I'm having with them is going to be resolved soon, maybe before you leave Moscow. What I really need right now is to find that money, to open up my own business by myself. If I could start my own optician business now, I'd be earning more money than any other optician in Moscow. I have the best connections. I know where to get everything. I know all the optician's stores in Moscow and Leningrad. I haven't been working very long, but I work everyday. I know where to find everything I need—what lenses are available, how much they cost, how to find this or that. So it's as if I'd already been working for five years.

If you come to my business to see me, you'll see that the only thing I do there is take orders. Just the practical work. Then I take the orders to the technicians. But if I were working by myself, could do as I wanted, I would set up the tools right there, at our booth, and bring the technician there. I would like to do that.

I had to begin with those "co-founders" because I started out selling surplus glasses. I couldn't have just stood there on the street, selling by myself. I needed someone to help me. And I felt sorry for Misha, his wife was pregnant and he needed work, and then Zhenya, the second one, had just come back from the army and didn't have any work. And I thought they were friends so that it would work out. I showed them the ropes. But now I'm the one who is trying to survive!

THE ARMY

I didn't serve in the army. I went to the hospital, and pretended that I was ill. So they ran all kinds of tests on me. I told them quite a story, a real drama, I painted some picture! I made myself look like I was suffering, what a face! So they put me in a hospital for tests, they did all kinds of analyses, with computers, but I was able to fool the computers! I hope this doesn't end up in Russian newspapers! I filled my mouth with water, to fool the computers, the neurological ones, to make it seem that there was really something wrong with my head. You fill your mouth with water and hide your tongue someplace in your cheeks, you close your eyes even though they tell you that you're not supposed to close your eyes while you're having the test done. That's how I fooled the computers and didn't go into the army.

And two more of my friends did the same thing. And they got out for the same reasons, some kind of deviation in the head, something really wrong, with the blood pressure, or something, or inflammation of the brain tissue. I read a lot of books before I went into those exams. I read everything I could find about headaches, problems with the head, blood pressure, and I started thinking about it. How can I manage to do this? How does that computer work? How can I fool the computer? I knew that if I had my eyes closed, it would be a full sphere, and if I had one eye opened, it would be half a sphere. It's a whole, complicated story. I learned a lot about this though. I learned how to make my blood pressure go up.

More than half the guys who are supposed to go to the army do things like this. I can tell from my own acquaintances. I can tell you that of all my friends, not even one went into the army! One friend fooled the doctors, another packed his bags and left for Israel—he didn't go to emigrate, he just went for a while, hoping that they would forget about him in the army. Actually he's returning any day now. What's there for him to do there? It turned out that it's difficult to live here, but it's difficult to live there, too. You have to be able to find some kind of little job, here or there. At least here there are some ways to do that now. In any case, he doesn't have to worry. By now they've forgotten about him in the army. Nobody's going to come after him.

Things have changed a lot concerning the army. Parents used to say, "If you don't serve, you won't be a real man." And now they say, "What would you go into that Army for? You'll just lose the best years of your life." Anybody who has any kind of understanding is going through a change of view now. My parents have gotten a lot more relaxed in the way they view all this commerce. Before they couldn't stand it. They think differently about young people now too. And I remember how much they wanted me to go into the army before! Everything was okay as long as I went to the army. And now they are glad I didn't go. Really glad. They've changed their attitudes about my being in commerce as well. Now they say, "Go ahead, get involved with whatever you want. Please. Do whatever you want to." It's more than two years that I haven't had to take any money from my parents. I live off my own money and they like that. They like the fact that I'm independent.

THE CURRENT SITUATION

During the last two years I've had this feeling, as I sit in the metro, as I'm going someplace, that I'm continuing the story I began to tell you then, I'm continuing the book. I think, "This is good, this is bad." I realize that I've started to relate to everything differently from the way I did before. Now some of my friends and I have been thinking that we should write a book called "Children of the Caves," about the children of these hungry times! You know, a cave, a hole in the earth!

At the beginning of perestroika I supported Gorbachev. But then I started to have doubts because by then it was clear

that something wasn't right, that he was doing some things
that just weren't right. Okay, thanks to him he opened up all
these roads to the West, the roads to commerce, but that's
all. The country has entered a state of chaos now, and what
he started to do is what other people are continuing to
do now! Since August, Yeltsin. But I think the coup happened because they all made some sort of agreements
among themselves.

The first day, when I found out that there had been a
coup, I remember thinking, "My God, what is going to happen now? They're going to isolate us completely, close off all
the doors to other countries, close off all these commercial
ties, all commerce." I ran as fast as I could to Moscow. I live
by the Ring Road, and you can still see to this day how torn
up the road is from the tanks.* I saw a whole column of
tanks. And in the morning you could see that near every
metro station there were tanks, soldiers everywhere. There
were people who were happy about this. But by evening I had
found the people who were distributing leaflets against the
coup, supporting Gorbachev, Yeltsin, trying to get people to
have a meeting near our White House. I grabbed a whole
bunch of the leaflets and all night, even when the curfew
started, I was gluing up those leaflets all through my neighborhood, everywhere I could. I used up two big cans of glue.

So there was a coup, and now this coup is continuing right
up to this day! Because Yeltsin came to power, and he raised
prices and every month prices continue to rise! The day
before yesterday there was a rumor that yesterday prices
would go up by 70 percent, for everything. Maybe things did
go up a little, but everybody believed the rumor and immedi-

---

*The Ring Road is a highway that circles the outer border of the
Moscow city limits. Many of the tanks summoned to Moscow to stage the
August coup traveled along parts of the Ring Road. The fact that Alexei's
neighborhood is located near the Ring Road is indicative of how distant it
is from the center.

ately started running around trying to buy things. Several people told me about it. The minute people hear anything about prices going up or about money being changed, they take off and run to stores!

People just don't believe in the government. I don't believe in Yeltsin. When he first came to power it was clear that it was all planned in advance—Gorbachev leaving office, the switch to Yeltsin. Yeltsin is the winner. As soon as the coup was over, he started talking about the bad ones in office, the ones over there, etc., etc. People respected him. He wanted to raise himself in the public's eye, and he managed to do just that. But he's doing the same thing they were doing. Even worse. The old ones in power were against raising prices! But Yeltsin raised them! Two, three, ten times! But salaries have only gone up two times. And so practically 70 percent of the population in Moscow lives below the poverty line! We were a country of fools and now we are a country of beggars! And I'm surprised by how the people I know are reacting to this. In any other country—well, in Germany, for example—they made them raise salaries 40 percent. And there were strikes.

I've changed in every way in the last three years. All my views of life have changed because of what I've done and what I've seen. I'm living through a very complicated time. Terrible. I'm unlucky. Because before everything was simple and clear. In the 1940s and 1950s, then it was clear: if somebody was your enemy, he was your enemy. Now everybody's your enemy, but they all say they're your friend. It's hard to figure things out. But people just look at all of this, as if they've just been bowled over by something. Like somebody said to them, "You're living badly now? Well, wait till next month, you'll be living even worse." And people say okay! And look, it is getting worse, every month prices go up and people live worse. And nobody says anything about it, they just ignore it. Or maybe one or two people say something. Not like during the coup.

Nobody could be satisfied with what is going on here now. I don't think there are people who are really optimistic, who believe that something is going to come of all this. Because things are going to get even worse. I think the price increases are going to go on until the end of August. But what will be after that, I don't know. Maybe another coup, like there was last year. The coup was really the same thing as perestroika. They tell us the same thing: "Give us the power, we'll do everything for you. Just endure this for a little while longer. Everything will be okay." Well, people have been enduring! And there's nowhere left to go anymore. Such a crisis. And then somebody new comes to power and says, "Just be patient, just hold on a little longer, I'll take care of everything for you. Just endure this another half year." So half a year goes by, people take it. And what happens? Look what's going on here! Since 1985! From the beginning of perestroika. Everybody's "enduring." And what will happen? Well, we'll need to write a whole other book to talk about that, in another five years!

The only reason why people protested during the coup was because of all the tanks they sent into Moscow. If they hadn't sent in tanks, nobody would have done anything. People would have just gone on living the way they were. People just couldn't take those tanks, so they stood up in protest. For the most part people here just stand for everything. No matter how bad things are, they just take it. If you make things worse, they'll just stand for that, too! But that moment does arrive when people can't take it anymore and they revolt. I think anybody here could end up at the barricades. Anybody. Like during the coup. But a lot of people didn't even know about it—my neighbors, for example. At the time of the coup they showed some old movie on TV, a black-and-white movie about thirty years old, so people wouldn't know what was going on.

Things certainly haven't gotten any better for young people in the sense of having things to do, people have gotten

involved with crime. Crime has grown more than anything
else around here. Speculation. That's what young people are
getting involved with. Like my friends. More than half of my
schoolmates, from before I went into the PTU, drink. They're
alcoholics. One has gotten involved with karate. Another
stayed in the army and became an officer. One is working
with me at the optician's. One went to the university. One is
working. Another one has been is prison for four years and
he's going to be there for a long time. He killed someone.

FAMILY LIFE

Last year when I worked as a fireman, I made some arrange-
ments and managed to buy a very good chicken on my way to
work, a great chicken, and now for a year and a half I've got a
great chicken coop, about a ten-minute walk from my house,
and we've got fresh eggs every morning! It's right next to our
house! Actually we've got five garden plots. We used to have
three, from way back when, and now we've bought two more.
The family bought them, near our dacha. We had to buy
them—after all, the family's gotten bigger now, three times as
big. My sister and her big family, now she's just given birth to
a second child, and my aunt got married, and of course
someday I think I'll get married too.

My mother was laid off from her job. She was a teacher of
Russian but she left that job and became an English translator for the firm Rano. A fairly prestigious firm, still Soviet
when she worked there. They delivered x-ray equipment to
other countries, to Mongolia, to Afghanistan. She took that
job when she returned from Africa. She worked for the government before she went to Africa, but when she returned to
Moscow, she hadn't been at that job for years and there was
somebody who had replaced her, who had been working
there for five years already. They didn't need her anymore.
So she took this other job, and she became pretty well known

there. I can tell because they still call her for advice: "How do you do this, translate this or that?" She understood all the papers that came their way. But they laid her off because the company went bankrupt. They didn't have any money to pay salaries. They laid off more than half the people who worked there! They left every second person, so that he could do the work of two! And they fired them without any kind of compensation. They just said you have to leave by such and such a date, and that was it. Two months ago.

Right now she's just doing some free-lance translations from English. She's looking for work. She types book manuscripts for a publishing house. Little jobs. What she earns doesn't even stretch enough to pay for bread!

My father earns 1,000, 1,500 rubles at work now, at his institute. I'm the only one who's earning anything in our family at the moment.

We haven't had any sugar in our family for three weeks. We were using little candies to sweeten things. But they got used up, too, and fortunately I was able to find some sugar, but I paid a fantastic sum for it! Muscovites eat a lot of sugar! And that's the most painful point here—sugar used to cost 70 kopecks and now it costs 70 rubles. A hundred times more expensive! Now if they would only raise salaries a hundred times, would I ever be earning a lot of money! Last year, when sugar cost 70 kopecks, the average salary was 500 or 600 rubles. So if salaries went up a hundred times, I would be earning 50,000 or 60,000 a month! But we don't get anything near that. So they raised the price of sugar a hundred times, and it's going to go up more, to 140 rubles a kilo, and how much did they raise salaries? Ten times, at the most. The country is going hungry. I know people, personally, who are practically feeding themselves from the garbage, from things that people have thrown away. Acquaintances of mine whom I know pretty well go around to cafeterias and pick up the leftovers, but Muscovites are proud people and they would never tell you that they were eating leftovers. But I've heard them. "Look what good dough we've found! We'll make *bliny** out of it!" But they would never admit that they found the batter in a cafeteria, that it had been thrown away. The cafeteria had thrown it away because they didn't know what to do with it, it was going to rot. So my friends took a rag, wiped it off, cleaned it up, they added a little water to it, and they made *bliny*, and they ate them. Same thing with bread. They go around to cafeterias and take what's been thrown away. Nobody would do that before! They'd go to a bakery and buy bread for 17 kopecks! And you know what bread costs now?

THE PARTY

My parents left the Party before the beginning of the end of the Party. They left when they returned from Africa. They had to join the Party in order to work abroad. They never let people who weren't in the Party travel. But my parents never supported the Party, never really believed in it. They joined it to begin with because it was the only way to travel.

I spoke well of the Party in the book because I was young. I didn't even know that my great-great-grandfather was a staff officer for General Antonov.[†] And that my father's parents were sent into exile. They were all pretty solid people, and it seems that after the Revolution, in the 1920s, they were all sent to Siberia. And my great-grandfather took my grandfather away to Tula—they ran away, they hid. That's why my parents never had a good relationship to the Party, but of course, they never said anything to me about it. Really, they

---

*Thin pancakes, a typical Russian dish, similar to crepes.

[†]A well-known leader of the White Guard of the White Army, which fought the Red Army during the Civil War following the October Revolution. In this discussion of his relatives and their history, Alexei is trying to convey that his family, rather than being loyal Party members as he stated three years ago, actually has deep roots in the opposition to the Bolshevik Revolution and to the Soviet government.

were even afraid that our apartment was bugged, that people were listening. They're still afraid of the same thing. The KGB hasn't really disappeared. I know. I heard that as many bugs as they had planted, as much as they spied on people, they still do. People just don't know about it. They only write about it to a certain extent.

PLANS

I suppose I wish I could study. I wish I could become somebody other than the person I have become, having finished a PTU. If I had at least finished the technical school,* I would be the boss of the guys who finished the PTU with me. But I didn't graduate from that technical school, I finished the PTU, and in any case I'm not working in this field or in that one, and that's just the way my life turned out. I've been successful in that I freed myself from the army and I freed myself from the hard labor that I was supposed to do after the PTU. Now I work where I want to, not where they sent me. And it's not that they didn't force me to work there. They did, but I ran away. I simply disappeared. They went looking for me, but I didn't show up. They phoned me at home, they showed up at my house, and I hid. Everybody hid me, too, they all told them, "Alexei's not here. We don't know where he is." And that was that. I said to my mother, "Mom, I'm not going to work there! I'm going to work as a fireman." And my mother said, "Okay then, I'll tell them you're not here."

I don't think it would have been any different if I had graduated five years earlier, before perestroika. I've always been interested in selling things. I've always had commercial inclinations. I've always loved doing things like that, always loved having nice, beautiful things, that's why I never really could

---

*The school in which Alexei had enrolled for one year before dropping out and going into the PTU from which he graduated.

have worked as a carpenter. When I did, I felt so embarrassed about wearing those work pants. I just couldn't get myself to wear them. I like to wear fashionable clothes. Maybe if I'm working in the garden, Okay, I can dress like that, but not every day! If I had to wear those work pants every day, I'd be running around red-faced! I wouldn't want anybody to see me! But I do think sixteen-year-olds now are very different from the way we were. It's possible that they know some things we didn't—for example, about video recorders and players, and they use new words, a different slang already—but they know less about life than we do. That's the way older generations always talk about younger ones, but in this case it's true. They don't feel like doing anything. They're not interested in anything.

Sometimes I really feel like getting married and having kids and other times I don't. Boys right over there in America, they don't want to get married so early. But the truth is that I really feel older than I am, about six years older. All my friends are older than I am. And I've already been through so much that most young men my age haven't seen yet, can't even imagine! I'm already dying for some peace and quiet. I'm ready to retire! Someplace quiet, in the countryside. I've worked so much already. I'm just barely hanging in there.

I do have someone already—maybe I'll marry her. I met her right before I went to America, and since then I've been getting together with her every day. She works in the diplomatic *beriozka** as the chief salesperson there. They sell for hard currency now but they're going to start selling for rubles.

I might get married, but I might not. Because the way life has turned out in this country, in order to have a wedding,

---

*Beriozka shops were hard-currency shops, and off-limits to the average Soviet citizen. Working in one carried a certain prestige because of the access it gave to imported and otherwise scarce goods. Many of these shops have closed or have started to sell goods for rubles as well.

you have to put aside at least 20,000 rubles. And if my family brings in 2,000 a month, it means you have to save a year's money just to have a wedding! And the bride's wedding dress costs 15,000. You won't spend less than 30,000 for the whole thing. A whole year of income just to have a wedding! And to have a baby—the birth costs 4,000 or 5,000. Medicine costs money now. Almost everything costs money these days. There's hardly anything that's free anymore. Kindergartens always cost money, but what did people pay? Thirty rubles a month, and now 160. And in our neighborhood they're getting ready to close the kindergartens because they don't have anything to feed the kids! They're sending kids home to their parents. I don't know what the parents are supposed to do. My sister's kid's kindergarten had to borrow 20,000 rubles from another kindergarten just to feed the kids for three days. Parents send what they can to the kindergarten to help out. I spend days thinking about what is happening here. What will be? How in the world can we fix the situation we've gotten into?

"A FAMILY WITHOUT A CHILD IS LIKE A PERSON WITHOUT ARMS OR LEGS"

NATASHA

Nineteen years old, third-year student at a teacher training college

Natasha has gotten married and is pregnant. At three months she is still rail-thin. She looks much like the same teenage Natasha I knew three years ago: neat, proper, a modest appearance. Hearing her news, I am shocked that she is expecting a baby. She looks so young to me that it is hard to imagine that soon she will have a child. But Natasha entertains no doubts. She is tired but she is very excited and completely confident.

While I am in Moscow she is busy with final exams. She has many things going on in her life and is able to meet with me only once. We plan a second meeting at Tanya's apartment–the two young women are in the same college–but Natasha calls that morning to say that she will not be coming. She has promised a friend to find a certain medication in scarce supply, and in order to do that she must make a complicated rendezvous in the afternoon. "That is how we do things around here," she tells me. "I know everything is simpler in your country. Please understand."

We finish the interview in an hour-long phone call a few days later. Natasha is far more interested in talking about her baby than she is in talking about the teacher-training college and her career. I remember how certain Natasha was three years ago that she would

NATASHA

become a teacher. But now something far more urgent awaits her:
motherhood.

I don't know if I really am going to work as a teacher. I don't
like our school system, and I've had the chance to see a lot of
schools since I started studying at the college. The atmosphere in our schools is bad, the relations between teachers
are bad, and the relations between teachers and the administration are bad. And all this affects the way teachers relate to
their students. I think most of the administrators, the principals and assistant principals, are part of the older generation,
and they can't do anything new.

I might be interested in working in one of the new gymna-
siums.* I know of about six of them. I think that's where
teachers have some freedom to use new methods. But so far
schools in general haven't been affected by change. And I
think until the older generation of teachers and administrators leaves the schools, nothing will change. They write that
the schools are changing, but I don't think they are. I want to
work with children, but not in that authoritarian atmosphere,
in a bad collective.

I've been in a lot of schools and seen all this myself
because we have a lot of practical work in our college. I can't
say that I've been very impressed by the schools I've seen. I
keep reading that Russians are well-read people and that we
have a high level of knowledge in Russia, but I haven't seen
that. I don't think it's true. Part of it depends upon where you
went to secondary school. I have some friends who finished
special schools, the elite schools, and have now gotten into
the university. But even they are disappointed with what

---

*Several new types of schools have emerged in the last few years. The
contemporary gymnasium is based on the type of school with the same
name that existed in tsarist Russia. Its curriculum includes a wide variety of
academic courses, particularly in the humanities, that do not exist in the
current secondary education curriculum.

they're finding there. Not just in the university either, but different prestigious institutes, like the Moscow Aviation Institute, the Institute for Foreign Relations, places like that.

I think they tried to get students to enroll in our college by making the advertisements seem really attractive, but those advertisements were at least 80 percent false. I'm really disappointed. They made a lot of promises they can't fulfill. We're getting only part of our higher education there. We're supposed to be able to complete our higher education by getting into an institute, like the pedagogical institute. But now we're finding out that the institutes don't want to take us! We're just supposed to get out there and find a job, but I enrolled at that college thinking that I would begin my studies there and then complete my higher education someplace else.

This year we had three teachers who got sick and couldn't teach their courses. And they didn't even find any substitutes. We just didn't have the classes. So our group leader tried to speak to the administration about this but nothing happened. One student was even expelled from the school because he went to the administration to complain about something.

Our director, Tamara Nikolayevna, is a former deputy of the former Soviet Union. I've seen her at the most four or five times per year. She's almost never there. Her assistant is the one who takes care of all the school business. The relationships in the college are bad, and that's part of what makes the whole place so bad. I remember when I was in secondary school, our principal would stand there right in the doorway to greet students at the beginning of each school day. And for me, that was a living person, a real person! But at the college, with the exception of three or four people, nobody has any character for me. Only three or four are interesting and know how to teach.

But I'm going to finish studying there, and I'd like to be accepted at a pedagogical institute and finish my higher education. I'm not going to continue right away—I just want to finish the college and take my exams next year, and then I'll stop for now. I'm going to have a baby in November and I want to stay home with my child for five years, which is the maximum amount of paid leave you can get here now.* I've seen the kindergartens, the nursery schools we have here, and I don't want my child to go to one of those!

If you had asked me about this two years ago, I would have said something different. I would have said that I'd like to spend one year at home. But now that I've seen what I've seen in the schools, my opinion has changed. I don't want my child's personality to be damaged in one of our nurseries!

I'm going to try to get the college to let me take my exams early next year, in the middle of the year instead of at the end, because of the baby. I'd like to be able to finish college with the group I started out with, because I like my collective there. There are twenty-seven people in it—twenty-five girls and two boys! I think the group from the year after mine is weaker, and so I don't want to have to finish with them. Those two boys didn't make it through though. One left, and the other one got kicked out. He's the one who went to the administration to complain. I would have left, too, except that I will have put three years into my studies there, and I don't want to lose those three years. And in five years, after I've spent that time with my child, I'd like to go back to work, or study.

MARRIAGE

I met my husband Andrei on January 4 and got married on March 27. We didn't know each other very well, but we really

---

*Maternity leave was recently extended from three to five years. Ironically, increasing financial hardship for much of the population renders this extension almost meaningless. Maternity pay is so low that even before the rapidly increasing inflation it was difficult to take advantage of the leave. Now, for most women, it is simply impossible.

fell in love. He has a golden head, and golden hands! I really didn't expect anything like this to happen to me. I remember when something like this happened to a friend of mine, she just met somebody and fell in love and got married, and I told her that it was too fast. But now look! It's happened to me, too.

Andrei, by training, restores antiques, old furniture. But he's not working in that now. He's working with my father, who started his own business. Dad's a construction worker. He was a foreman before, for years, and he's a very skilled worker. So they've started a business and they construct all kinds of buildings. They built some cottages for some people from the KGB, and they've built things for other rich people, too. So they make good money. In one week they can make 20,000 rubles! That's 10,000 each! Somehow they ended up with a "family clan" at work!

Mom doesn't earn very much at her job, though, just about 2,000 a month. And my grandmother doesn't earn much, either.

We're all living together now, and our home situation is good. There are five of us, in a three-room apartment, but we like living together. In our circumstances, it's easier for everybody to live together, to help each other out. And I like living with my parents. We all get along very well together. Andrei and I have one room—and the baby, of course, will be with us—my parents another, and my grandmother lives in the third.

My baby's due at the end of November. I got pregnant sometime in February. But that's not why we got married! We knew we wanted a child right away, and we made one! Because it seems to me that a family without a child is like a person without arms or legs. And now I'm growing impatient. It seems to take such a long time! I just can't wait for this baby to be born!

Even with everything so difficult right now, with food and things like that, I'm not having a hard time. In the first place, we have a lot of money at the moment. And also there's a good store in my neighborhood. It was privatized last year and the workers bought it. There's plenty of food in that store. And we buy meat, which I need right now, at the farmer's market, even though it's so expensive.

In each district it's different. Some neighborhoods have better clinics and special stores that have things like milk and meat especially for pregnant women. We've got a good clinic in our neighborhood. So I'm doing fine.

THE CURRENT SITUATION

In the last year I've become very disinterested in politics. After the coup I was conscious, active. I demonstrated. But now I feel that I have been deceived. Nothing good has come out of this. And I don't understand what's going on. All this ethnic strife that's become so widespread—I really don't understand how it happened, and so fast. Just a few years ago, people got along! And I'm really disturbed by the attitude toward Russians that is developing in the Baltic republics. So much hostility. And I always thought so highly of the people in the Baltic. Now they behave so badly toward Russians, so much ill will, and they're depriving Russians of their rights.

Everybody's complaining about high prices all the time. But that's really nothing. Compared to the wars and the killing, who cares about high prices? These wars have to stop! This is what really affects me the most. To kill another person, to take somebody else's life, is the worst sin there is. I don't even think it matters whose fault it is. It simply has to stop! But I don't think things will go on this way. People will get themselves together. I think that something will happen here like what is happening in the European common market. Maybe we'll be able to do the same here, after we've taken a rest from each other for a while! But still, I'm discouraged. I really do have the feeling that I've been fooled.

I've changed in other ways, too. I started to believe in God. But not the way they formulate him. The point isn't religion—whether you're a Protestant, Catholic, Buddhist. There is a God, and there's one God for everybody.

And then I realized that I have a "third eye." I'm able to help take away people's pains. Headaches, and things like that. It has to do with people's biopoles. Every person has one. I can use my hands and have an effect on a person's bio-pole. People come to me and ask me to help them. I use my hands, there's a kind of force I have within me, and I help cure them of their aches and pains. But it takes a lot of ener-gy from me, and even though I've been told that during preg-nancy this strength of mine will grow even stronger, I'm not using it at the moment precisely because I am pregnant. It takes too much out of me. It could be harmful. But actually, I don't want to talk about this too much. I don't think it's a good idea to talk about it.

"I HOPE MY LIFE WILL
HAVE SOME MEANING"

KATYA

*Nineteen years old, third-year student in the Economics
Department of the Moscow Aviation Institute*

*I meet Katya outside her building on a warm, sunny afternoon. She
seems happy to see me, but maintains a polite, almost shy reserve.
She has become a poised young woman, thick hair pulled neatly
back, dressed in a white, lined blazer, cream-colored blouse, and a
print skirt in tones of brown and yellow, all of which she has sewn
herself. She wears low pumps and stockings.*

*We stand in the driveway that leads to the front of her building.
Katya's mother and little brother Andryusha emerge from the building. They greet us and get inside a waiting car. It is Friday and
they are heading for the dacha. But since I am in town this week,
Katya stays behind. Knowing how Muscovites love to escape the big
city on the weekend–and when possible, for the whole summer–I
appreciate her decision to remain just to spend time with me.*

*Katya is a college student; decisions about the future are several
years away. She's living at home, does not have to work. Her family's financial situation is precarious, but they are making ends
meet. There have been no great changes in Katya's personal life.
And she, more than anyone else, seems calm and relaxed.*

KATYA

While I was still finishing tenth grade I started taking preparatory classes* at the Moscow Aviation Institute. I knew it was a good institute, that the education you get there is of high quality—at least that's the reputation it's always had, and that's where my parents got their degrees. I knew that they had good preparatory classes there and I decided to attend because I knew that the school curriculum we have in mathematics and physics wouldn't give me the knowledge I needed to be accepted. So I finished the courses, and I liked the institute a lot. It's very pleasant, the atmosphere and the teachers are good. As soon as I finished the courses I took the entrance exams. They had a system there—at the end of the courses you took final exams, but those exams were also considered the entrance exams to the institute. So I was accepted in May, before I even graduated from school. And then afterwards I took the exams in school, to graduate!

The first year there I just took general courses. There are nine departments at the institute, but the first year everybody studies the same general courses, takes the same exams, and then you go ahead and choose what you want to study. But there was something I didn't like about that system, because the exams you took in the first year were designed to get as many students as possible to fail. They were written exams, and I would prepare according to the lectures of one teacher, the one I had been studying with, but the person who corrected my exam was somebody else. And that teacher would have different demands and expectations. A lot of students failed their exams because of that. I think that if I work with one teacher, that's the person whose questions I should answer. But in the second year we had a more normal approach to that.

---

*Many institutions of higher education have preparatory classes to help students in their final year of secondary school prepare for the difficult, competitive entrance exams. Most secondary-school students who are determined to be accepted in a particular institute will spend considerable time in their final year of school preparing for these entrance exams.

After the first year the students choose the department they're going to study in. I went to the Economics Department. But actually the real specializations begin with the third year, this coming year for me. Of course it's very different in my department from the Department of Airplane Construction! Although actually we did go to a factory a few times, where airplanes are built—we went and touched the airplanes, felt them, looked at them. After all, we do study in the Aviation Institute!

But I would like there to be some other kinds of courses, too. Even though I'm studying in a technically oriented institute, I would like some other kinds of courses. Like literature. I like literature, ancient history, of course contemporary history—well, I'll never understand that! But unfortunately we don't have courses like that in a technically oriented institute. If I wanted to study something like that, I would have to go to some other institute, get accepted, and start all over again.

Actually we did have history in our first year, but it was the same thing we had in school. The twentieth century, the Revolution, the same old thing, history of the Communist Party of the Soviet Union. They called it "Political History." There wasn't a feeling of anything new in that course.

To be honest, I myself am not sure why I've chosen this career. I think basically I'm a person with technical inclinations. I got that from my parents. That's why I went to a technically oriented VUZ, although it's true I like the humanities too. I've always liked literature and never had any problems with those kinds of subjects. But on the other hand I can't say that I am such a technical person that I could, for example, devote myself entirely to mathematics. I was thinking about that for a while, going to the Mathematics Department, but I think it's a good thing I didn't. I chose economics in the first place because, after all, it's the kind of profession that's really necessary right now, and—well, I'm not sure why things turned out this way. I don't know exactly what I'll do with a degree in economics.

Economics wasn't a very popular field in the past, but it's gotten more interesting. Before, there was just one kind of economics: planned. Now all kinds of different courses are appearing. A lot of people are going to want to study economics. New courses are appearing, more men now want to study economics. About half the students in my department are women, half men. In the other departments of the institute where I study, students have always been predominantly male. In a group of fifteen students, maybe three or four women. But in economics it was always just the opposite because it wasn't a very popular field. Maybe only three or four men. But that's changing now. Men are starting to go into economics. But the competition to get into the economics department still isn't as tough as in the other departments, where it's really difficult.

I like economics. I'm glad I chose to do that. And I like the teachers too. In our class in political economy we don't have a fixed syllabus, this or that or the other. The teacher can come up with her own program. And she gives us lectures and then, since it's a seminar, we all sit around and discuss this with her. Like price formation. She recommends things from journals or newspapers on economics. We talk about what's going on in this country, but only during class time. Among ourselves we don't really talk that much about those things. We talk about things that happen to us daily, about friends. But not about politics! If we talk about politics, it's not very often. Sometimes we'll say to each other, "Ooo, that Yeltsin!"—we don't like him that much.

CHANGES IN THE FAMILY

One could say that in my family it's gotten much harder to live because of where my parents work—in arms production. Their situation at work has gotten really difficult. Especially where Mom works, at a scientific research institute connected with arms production. Of course they haven't started firing people yet, they're still producing, but they're in such a moment of great transition, when something has to change, and probably not for the better. There's a kind of crisis now at her workplace. The financial situation there is very bad; they're not getting paid regularly, and what they do get is very low pay. I think they haven't even gotten all of April's pay yet, not to mention May, and here we are at the beginning of June. I'm not sure what my Dad's salary is, but Mom's is about 840 rubles and they haven't even paid her all of that. I try to buy very little and spend very little money. Almost all our money goes for food. I can't really let myself buy much of anything else. I get a student stipend—340 rubles a month. Two dollars!

Mom's really upset about what's going on right now. She thinks it's unjust, the way life is around here now. If you have money, you can do something. And people only do things nowadays if it will get them something or give them some advantage. Mom thinks it's unfair that people have ended up in the situation we're in. I don't know if she would go back to the pre-perestroika days or not. Life was easier then, that's why people say they would go back to those times.

You see, my parents worked, and worked, did what they loved doing, and now . . . Look, my Dad's a scientist, and the area he's been working in, arms production, has ended up being shoved aside. All his life he was working in the field he loved, they were always working on some new invention, and so from his point of view, despite the fact that his pay was always so low, well, how could he like what's going on these days? It's not even that my family ever had a lot, but now he doesn't have anything. A lot of people where he works, people with good heads, specialists, are leaving. They're losing a lot of people. It's really terrible.

But a person shouldn't go around all the time saying "This is bad, that is bad." Right now around here that's all you see. You turn on the television, and what do you see? "Everything's bad, everything's terrible." My grandmother is really suffering now. She's always in such a bad mood. She watches television all the time and we have to tell her to turn it off! She's always so pessimistic. We tell her that she can't go around thinking about nothing except how terrible things are. It simply becomes impossible to live. Thinking about that all the time. The other grandmother is in better health and she lives outside the city. She has her garden and now she's happy there, planting, her tomatoes, her cucumbers, she has all her plans. One can't start thinking only about politics! Life goes on, after all, and a person has to find a path somehow.

But even though in general the situation at their work is difficult, some new contracts are coming up, about to be signed, so we're hoping. People are holding on, because what else can you do? Mom wouldn't be able to find another job at the moment because she has the kind of specialization where it would be really difficult for a woman older than forty to get a job. She's an engineer. She graduated from the Department of Radio Technology. She wouldn't be able to find another job now. So she doesn't have any other choice but to sit it out, be patient, wait. The situation of women who are near forty or over forty has gotten worse. Things are really difficult for them. They're not considered young women here, and it's become very hard for them to find work unless they've got connections or friends someplace. Where Mom works, a lot of specialists have left, have gone to look for work in other places. Basically, the only people who are left are women—older women, past forty. They don't really have the opportunity to find work someplace else and they're just waiting. I think there's even an unemployment bureau that's been established just for women. Mom doesn't think she'd find work anyplace else. She's not even looking! She doesn't have energy to do that. She's not in the frame of mind to look. She's got other problems. My brother Andryusha is growing up, she's got to spend time with him, and then there's the dacha, and that takes a lot of time.

So we have some difficulties now in our family, but we're
hanging in there. We go to the dacha. That's our travel. And
that's the thing that saves us—what we ourselves plant. The
potatoes we planted saved us last year. The things we get
from our garden get us through the winter. There are
moments when there's simply nothing to eat, and the stores
you have from what you've grown yourself are what save you.

POLITICS

Three years ago things seemed brighter, more full of hope.
And it seemed that everybody was so full of energy, that
everybody was going to really take their place, everything was
going to get put in order, like our guys won and now we're
going to really do something! But the people's level wasn't
up to that, not here.

Dad began to understand what the Party really was even
before Yeltsin banned it. By the time the ban came, he was
indifferent, he already felt no attachment to the Party. He
had begun to care only about what he himself was involved
in, his work. But people in general have started to worship
Yeltsin. I've met a lot of people like that who simply can't
approach the whole question rationally. Whatever Yeltsin
says is wonderful. Maybe that's a characteristic of people
around here. But Yeltsin came up through that same Party,
his whole life was spent in it!

When Dad was watching all those congresses, listening to
those speeches—well, he's fully able to separate what's true
from what's nonsense. And then, when everybody was flee-
ing from the Party, Dad had a different position. Perhaps it's
a little vulgar to put it this way, but it was something like the
expression that says "Only rats abandon a sinking ship." He
thought it was wrong at that precise moment of need, of crisis, to just run away, as if that were some great gesture—oh
yes, you democrats, you're so great. He couldn't just run
away like that. He thought it would be wrong. It's not a ques-

tion of his hanging on to his ideals or anything like that, that he's such a die-hard communist. No, he understood everything perfectly well and was well-oriented in the situation, but he just thought he should not behave in that way.

I don't know what Dad thinks about this transition to capitalism. We just don't talk about that topic. We have different problems now to talk about, more urgent daily problems, like the ones they are having at work. I don't know if what we really want to do around here is build capitalism, but we want to make our lives better. If capitalism will make our lives better, well then, okay, let's have capitalism. But I don't think we have to talk about "building" things right now. We just have to go on living.

It's hard to figure all this out, when things are changing so fast. It seems to me that you have to start with the little things, with yourself. A person has to work, get involved in his own work, the things he knows how to do well. In the first place I'll get something personally—some satisfaction—from that, and in the second place, I'll be doing something useful for society. It seems to me that the most important thing now is that everybody works, does something and does it well. That's the way we'll figure this out more quickly and get out of this difficult situation. I think we have some kind of optimism that things are going to get better, that things can't go on indefinitely like this. We're in such a black zone.

I don't know if my life will be complicated. I'm still in the process of preparing myself. But I'm preparing myself for things to be difficult! I hope my life will turn out all right, and I hope my life will have some meaning. It seems to me that it really depends on me.

Glossary

The reader may wish to consult the entries below for a better understanding of some political and educational terms that occur in the interviews.

Cooperatives. Cooperatives developed after the passage of a 1988 law permitting small-group private enterprises in the former USSR. At first most cooperatives were small ventures such as restaurants and cafés, and cooperatives were banned from such sectors such as the film industry, but they soon expanded into many other areas of the economy. In the educational arena cooperatives were initially limited to tutoring services and private lessons, but in post-Soviet Russia many of these restrictions have been lifted and private schools are now permitted. Since their inception, cooperatives have been a target of considerable popular resentment because of their higher prices and alleged "profiteering." Even though they are an accepted fact of life in Russia today, many people still believe that cooperatives earn their income through speculation and engaging in dishonest activities.

Glasnost (openness). A central policy of Mikhail Gorbachev's reform program, glasnost was intended to encourage freedom of expression and a general openness in the political, cultural, and intellectual life of the Soviet Union. One of the important accomplishments of the policy of glasnost was the suspension of most forms of state censorship. The result was a revolutionary change in the mass media and other sources of information. Many people argue that the lifting of censorship was ultimately responsible for the breakup of the Soviet

Union, since the party and other authority structures could not survive the massive wave of criticism that followed.

Perestroika (restructuring). Perestroika is the umbrella term for the comprehensive political, economic, and social reforms initiated by Mikhail Gorbachev and dating from shortly after his rise to leadership in March 1985 through the August 1991 coup. Gorbachev always stressed that the goal of his reforms was the renewal of the socialist order, which he proposed to accomplish through reduction of bureaucracy, decentralization of economic management, property reforms, the introduction of market mechanisms, and increased local autonomy. Political democratization and freedom of expression (**glasnost**) were important complements to the policy of perestroika. The breakup of the Soviet Union in 1992 marks the end of this tumultuous period of Soviet history, but its legacy is still felt in the developing new Russia.

Higher education. As used in Russia, the term **institute** generally refers to an institution of higher education other than a university. Both institutes and universities belong to the broad category of **institutions of higher education,** commonly known by the Russian acronym **VUZ** (vysshee uchebnoe zavedenie). **Colleges** (a direct borrowing from the English word) represent a movement to create new, more flexible institutions of higher education. Typically colleges are experimental and offer only "incomplete" degrees. For example, both Tanya and Natasha study at a new experimental college that trains primary school teachers (it offers a three-year course that is not equivalent to the degree earned at an institute). Traditionally, primary school teachers have been trained at technical schools which they entered after completing the ninth grade and which are not part of the system of higher education at all (see below).

Secondary education. Until recent times, the secondary education system has included three types of schools. **General academic secondary schools** prepare students to pursue a higher education. Other students are tracked into either **technical schools**, which train them for skilled technical positions in such fields as health care and primary education, or **vocational schools** (commonly known by their Russian acronym, **PTU**), in which students are trained to work in blue-collar production jobs immediately upon graduation. Recent attempts to decentralize the educational system have led to the appearance of new types of secondary schools. One of these is the **gymnasium**, modeled on the type of school with the same name which existed in tsarist Russia. The curriculum of the **gymnasium** features a wide variety of academic courses, particularly in the humanities, that are not generally included in the current secondary education curriculum.

Index

About the Author

Deborah Adelman lives in Chicago and teaches at the College of DuPage. She holds degrees from the University of Wisconsin, the New School for Social Research, and New York University. Her first visit to the Soviet Union, as a student, took place in 1978, and she has returned frequently since then, traveling throughout the country. While living in Moscow as a participant in a faculty exchange during 1988-89, she conducted interviews that appear in *The "Children of Perestroika": Moscow Teenagers Talk About Their Lives and the Future* (M.E. Sharpe, 1991). On her most recent visit to Moscow in the summer of 1992, she had follow-up interviews with these same "children of perestroika," which are presented in this companion volume—*The "Children of Perestroika" Come of Age: Young People of Moscow Talk About Life in the New Russia.*